CHEAPER BY
THE DOZEN

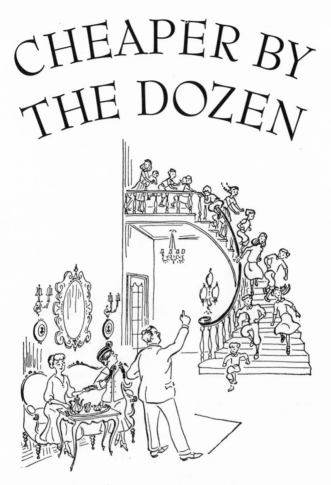

Frank B. Gilbreth, Jr.
and Ernestine Gilbreth Carey

Drawings by Vasiliu

📚 HarperCollins*Publishers*

This book was originally published in 1948 by Thomas Y. Crowell Company.

HarperCollins books may be purchased for educational, business, or sales promotional use. For information please write: Special Markets Department, HarperCollins Publishers, Inc., 10 East 53rd Street, New York, NY 10022.

Designed by George Nehrbas

LIBRARY OF CONGRESS CATALOG CARD NUMBER 63-20411

ISBN 0-690-18632-0

93 94 95 96 97 MV 10 9 8 7 6 5 4 3 2 1

To DAD
who only reared twelve children
and
To MOTHER
who reared twelve only children

Contents

Foreword   ix

1. *Whistles and Shaving Bristles*   1

2. *Pierce Arrow*   9

3. *Orphans in Uniform*   16

4. *Visiting Mrs. Murphy*   27

5. *Mister Chairman*   34

6. *Touch System*   43

7. *Skipping Through School*   59

8. *Kissing Kin*   74

9. *Chinese Cooking*   87

10. *Motion Study Tonsils*   96

11. *Nantucket*   114

12. *The* Rena   130

13. *Have You Seen the Latest Model?*   135

14. *Flash Powder and Funerals*   155

15. *Gilbreths and Company*   167

16. *Over the Hill*   188

17. *Four Wheels, No Brakes*   196

18. *Motorcycle Mac*   217

19. *The Party Who Called You . . .*   231

20. *And Many Years Later*   238

Foreword

Mother and Dad, Lillian Moller Gilbreth and Frank Bunker Gilbreth, were industrial engineers. They were among the first in the scientific management field and the very first in motion study. From 1910 to 1924, their firm of Gilbreth, Inc., was employed as "efficiency expert" by many of the major industrial plants in the United States, Britain, and Germany. Dad died in 1924. After that, Mother carried the load by herself and became perhaps the foremost woman industrial engineer. She is still active today after rearing twelve children. But that's another story. This book is about the Gilbreth family before Dad died.

CHAPTER 1

Whistles and Shaving Bristles

DAD was a tall man, with a large head, jowls, and a Herbert Hoover collar. He was no longer slim; he had passed the two-hundred-pound mark during his early thirties, and left it so far behind that there were times when he had to resort to railway baggage scales to ascertain his displacement. But he carried himself with the self-assurance of a successful gentleman who was proud of his wife, proud of his family, and proud of his business accomplishments.

Dad had enough gall to be divided into three parts, and the ability and poise to backstop the front he placed before the world. He'd walk into a factory like the Zeiss works in Germany or the Pierce Arrow plant in this country and announce that he could speed up production by one-fourth. He'd do it, too.

One reason he had so many children—there were twelve of us—

was that he was convinced anything he and Mother teamed up on was sure to be a success.

Dad always practiced what he preached, and it was just about impossible to tell where his scientific management company ended and his family life began. His office was always full of children, and he often took two or three of us, and sometimes all twelve, on business trips. Frequently, we'd tag along at his side, pencils and notebooks in our hands, when Dad toured a factory which had hired him as an efficiency expert.

On the other hand, our house at Montclair, New Jersey, was a sort of school for scientific management and the elimination of wasted motions—or "motion study," as Dad and Mother named it.

Dad took moving pictures of us children washing dishes, so that he could figure out how we could reduce our motions and thus hurry through the task. Irregular jobs, such as painting the back porch or removing a stump from the front lawn, were awarded on a low-bid basis. Each child who wanted extra pocket money submitted a sealed bid saying what he would do the job for. The lowest bidder got the contract.

Dad installed process and work charts in the bathrooms. Every child old enough to write—and Dad expected his offspring to start writing at a tender age—was required to initial the charts in the morning after he had brushed his teeth, taken a bath, combed his hair, and made his bed. At night, each child had to weigh himself, plot the figure on a graph, and initial the process charts again after he had done his homework, washed his hands and face, and brushed his teeth. Mother wanted to have a place on the charts for saying prayers, but Dad said as far as he was concerned prayers were voluntary.

It was regimentation, all right. But bear in mind the trouble most parents have in getting just one child off to school, and multiply it by twelve. Some regimentation was necessary to prevent bedlam. Of course there were times when a child would initial the charts without actually having fulfilled the requirements. However, Dad had a gimlet eye and a terrible swift sword. The combined effect was that truth usually went marching on.

Yes, at home or on the job, Dad was always the efficiency expert. He buttoned his vest from the bottom up, instead of from the top down, because the bottom-to-top process took him only three seconds, while the top-to-bottom took seven. He even used two shaving brushes to lather his face, because he found that by so doing he could cut seventeen seconds off his shaving time. For a while he tried shaving with two razors, but he finally gave that up.

"I can save forty-four seconds," he grumbled, "but I wasted two minutes this morning putting this bandage on my throat."

It wasn't the slashed throat that really bothered him. It was the two minutes.

Some people used to say that Dad had so many children he couldn't keep track of them. Dad himself used to tell a story about one time when Mother went off to fill a lecture engagement and left him in charge at home. When Mother returned, she asked him if everything had run smoothly.

"Didn't have any trouble except with that one over there," he replied. "But a spanking brought him into line."

Mother could handle any crisis without losing her composure.

"That's not one of ours, dear," she said. "He belongs next door."

None of us remembers it, and maybe it never happened. Dad wasn't above stretching the truth, because there was nothing he liked better than a joke, particularly if it were on him and even more particularly if it were on Mother. This much is certain, though. There were two red-haired children who lived next door, and the Gilbreths all are blondes or red heads.

Although he was a strict taskmaster within his home, Dad tolerated no criticism of the family from outsiders. Once a neighbor complained that a Gilbreth had called the neighbor's boy a son of an unprintable word.

"What are the facts of the matter?" Dad asked blandly. And then walked away while the neighbor registered a double take.

But Dad hated unprintable words, and the fact that he had stood up for his son didn't prevent him from holding a full-dress court of inquiry once he got home, and administering the called-for punishment.

Dad was happiest in a crowd, especially a crowd of kids. Wherever he was, you'd see a string of them trailing him—and the ones with plenty of freckles were pretty sure to be Gilbreths.

He had a way with children and knew how to keep them on their toes. He had a respect for them, too, and didn't mind showing it.

He believed that most adults stopped thinking the day they left school—and some even before that. "A child, on the other hand, stays impressionable and eager to learn. Catch one young enough," Dad insisted, "and there's no limit to what you can teach."

Really, it was love of children more than anything else that made him want a pack of his own. Even with a dozen, he wasn't fully satisfied. Sometimes he'd look us over and say to Mother:

"Never you mind, Lillie. You did the best you could."

We children used to suspect, though, that one reason he had

wanted a large family was to assure himself of an appreciative audience, even within the confines of the home. With us around, he could always be sure of a full house, packed to the galleries.

Whenever Dad returned from a trip—even if he had been gone only a day—he whistled the family "assembly call" as he turned in at the sidewalk of our large, brown home in Montclair. The call was a tune he had composed. He whistled it, loud and shrill, by doubling his tongue behind his front teeth. It took considerable effort and Dad, who never exercised if he could help it, usually ended up puffing with exhaustion.

The call was important. It meant drop everything and come running—or risk dire consequences. At the first note, Gilbreth children came dashing from all corners of the house and yard. Neighborhood dogs, barking hellishly, converged for blocks around. Heads popped out of the windows of near-by houses.

Dad gave the whistle often. He gave it when he had an important family announcement that he wanted to be sure everyone would hear. He gave it when he was bored and wanted some excitement with his children. He gave it when he had invited a friend home and wanted both to introduce the friend to the whole family and to show the friend how quickly the family could assemble. On such occasions, Dad would click a stopwatch, which he always carried in his vest pocket.

Like most of Dad's ideas, the assembly call, while something more than a nuisance, made sense. This was demonstrated in particular one day when a bonfire of leaves in the driveway got out of control and spread to the side of the house. Dad whistled, and the house was evacuated in fourteen seconds—eight seconds off the all-time record. That occasion also was memorable because of the remarks of a frank neighbor, who watched the blaze from his yard. During the height of the excitement, the neighbor's wife came to the front door and called to her husband:

"What's going on?"

"The Gilbreths' house is on fire," he replied, "thank God!"

"Shall I call the fire department?" she shouted.

"What's the matter, are you crazy?" the husband answered incredulously.

Anyway, the fire was put out quickly and there was no need to ask the fire department for help.

Dad whistled assembly when he wanted to find out who had been using his razors or who had spilled ink on his desk. He whistled it when he had special jobs to assign or errands to be run. Mostly, though, he sounded the assembly call when he was about to distribute some wonderful surprises, with the biggest and best going to the one who reached him first.

So when we heard him whistle, we never knew whether to expect good news or bad, rags or riches. But we did know for sure we'd better get there in a hurry.

Sometimes, as we all came running to the front door, he'd start by being stern.

"Let me see your nails, all of you," he'd grunt, with his face screwed up in a terrible frown. "Are they clean? Have you been biting them? Do they need trimming?"

Then out would come leather manicure sets for the girls and pocket knives for the boys. How we loved him then, when his frown wrinkles reversed their field and became a wide grin.

Or he'd shake hands solemnly all around, and when you took your hand away there'd be a nut chocolate bar in it. Or he'd ask who had a pencil, and then hand out a dozen automatic ones.

"Let's see, what time is it?" he asked once. Out came wrist watches for all—even the six-week-old baby.

"Oh, Daddy, they're just right," we'd say.

And when we'd throw our arms around him and tell him how we'd missed him, he would choke up and wouldn't be able to answer. So he'd rumple our hair and slap our bottoms instead.

CHAPTER 2

Pierce Arrow

THERE were other surprises, too. Boxes of Page and Shaw candy, dolls and toys, cameras from Germany, wool socks from Scotland, a dozen Plymouth Rock hens, and two sheep that were supposed to keep the lawn trimmed but died, poor creatures, from the combined effects of saddle sores, too much petting, and tail pulling. The sheep were fun while they lasted, and it is doubtful if any pair of quadrupeds ever had been sheared so often by so many.

"If I ever bring anything else alive into this household," Dad said, "I hope the Society for the Prevention of Cruelty to Animals hales me into court and makes me pay my debt to society. I never felt so ashamed about anything in my life as I do about those sheep. So help me."

When Dad bought the house in Montclair, he described it to us as a tumbled-down shanty in a run-down neighborhood. We thought this was another one of his surprises, but he finally convinced us that the house was a hovel.

"It takes a lot of money to keep this family going," he said. "Food, clothes, allowances, doctors' bills, getting teeth straightened, and buying ice cream sodas. I'm sorry, but I just couldn't afford anything better. We'll have to fix it up the best we can, and make it do."

We were living at Providence, Rhode Island, at the time. As we drove from Providence to Montclair, Dad would point to every termite-trap we passed.

"It looks something like that one," he would say, "only it has a few more broken windows, and the yard is maybe a little smaller."

As we entered Montclair, he drove through the worst section of town, and finally pulled up at an abandoned structure that even Dracula wouldn't have felt at home in.

"Well, here it is," he said. "Home. All out."

"You're joking, aren't you, dear?" Mother said hopefully.

"What's the matter with it? Don't you like it?"

"If it's what you want, dear," said Mother, "I'm satisfied. I guess."

"It's a slum, that's what's the matter with it," said Ernestine.

"No one asked your opinion, young lady," replied Dad. "I was talking to your Mother, and I will thank you to keep out of the conversation."

"You're welcome," said Ernestine, who knew she was treading on thin ice but was too upset to care. "You're welcome, I'm sure. Only I wouldn't live in it with a ten-foot pole."

"Neither would I," said Martha. "Not with two ten-foot poles."

"Hush," said Mother. "Daddy knows best."

Lill started to sob.

"It won't look so bad with a coat of paint and a few boards put in where these holes are," Mother said cheerfully.

Dad, grinning now, was fumbling in his pocket for his notebook.

"By jingo, kids, wait a second," he crowed. "Wrong address. Well, what do you know. Pile back in. I thought this place looked a little more run down than when I last saw it."

And then he drove us to 68 Eagle Rock Way, which was an old but beautiful Taj Mahal of a house with fourteen rooms, a two-story barn out back, a greenhouse, chicken yard, grape arbors, rose bushes, and a couple of dozen fruit trees. At first we thought that Dad was teasing us again, and that this was the other end of a scale—a house much better than the one he had bought.

"This is really it," he said. "The reason I took you to that other place first, and the reason I didn't try to describe this place to you is—well, I didn't want you to be disappointed. Forgive me?"

We said we did.

Dad had bought the automobile a year before we moved. It was our first car, and cars still were a novelty. Of course, that had been a surprise, too. He had taken us all for a walk and had ended up at a garage where the car had been parked.

Although Dad made his living by redesigning complicated machinery, so as to reduce the number of human motions required to operate it, he never really understood the mechanical intricacies of our automobile. It was a gray Pierce Arrow, equipped with two bulb horns and an electric Klaxon, which Dad would try to blow all at the same time when he wanted to pass anyone. The engine hood was long and square, and you had to raise it to prime the petcocks on cold mornings.

Dad had seen the car in the factory and fallen in love with it. The affection was entirely one-sided and unrequited. He named it Foolish Carriage because, he said, it was foolish for any man with as many children as he to think he could afford a horseless carriage.

The contraption kicked him when he cranked, spat oil in his face when he looked into its bowels, squealed when he mashed the brakes, and rumbled ominously when he shifted gears. Sometimes Dad would spit, squeal, and rumble back. But he never won a single decision.

Frankly, Dad didn't drive our car well at all. But he did drive it fast. He terrified all of us, but particularly Mother. She sat next to him on the front seat—with two of the babies on her lap—and alternated between clutching Dad's arm and closing her eyes in supplication. Whenever we rounded a corner, she would try to make a shield out of her body to protect the babies from what she felt sure would be mutilation or death.

"Not so fast, Frank, not so fast," she would whisper through clenched teeth. But Dad never seemed to hear.

Foolish Carriage was a right-hand drive, so whoever sat to the left of Mother and the babies on the front seat had to be on the lookout to tell Dad when he could pass the car ahead.

"You can make it," the lookout would shout.

"Put out your hand," Dad would holler.

Eleven hands—everybody contributing one except Mother and the babies—would emerge from both sides of the car; from the front seat, rear seat, and folding swivel chairs amidships. We had seen Dad nick fenders, slaughter chickens, square away with traffic policemen, and knock down full-grown trees, and we weren't taking any chances.

The lookout on the front seat was Dad's own idea. The other safety measures, which we soon inaugurated as a matter of self-preservation, were our own.

We would assign someone to keep a lookout for cars approaching on side streets to the left; someone to keep an identical lookout to the right; and someone to kneel on the rear seat and look through the isinglass window in the back.

"Car coming from the left, Dad," one lookout would sing out.

"Two coming from the right."

"Motorcycle approaching from astern."

"I see them, I see them," Dad would say irritably, although usually he didn't. "Don't you have any confidence at all in your father?"

He was especially fond of the electric horn, an ear-splitting gadget which bellowed "kadookah" in an awe-inspiring, metallic baritone. How Dad could manage to blow this and the two bulb horns, step on the gas, steer the car, shout "road hog, road hog," and smoke a cigar—all at the same time—is in itself a tribute to his abilities as a motion study expert.

A few days after he bought the car, he brought each of us children up to it, one at a time, raised the hood, and told us to look inside and see if we could find the birdie in the engine. While our backs were turned, he'd tiptoe back to the driver's seat—a jolly Santa Claus in mufti—and press down on the horn.

"Kadookah, Kadookah." The horn blaring right in your ear was frightening and you'd jump away in hurt amazement. Dad would laugh until the tears came to his eyes.

"Did you see the birdie? Ho, ho, ho," he'd scream. "I'll bet you jumped six and nine-tenths inches. Ho, ho, ho."

One day, while we were returning from a particularly trying picnic, the engine balked, coughed, spat, and stopped.

Dad was sweaty and sleepy. We children had gotten on his nerves. He ordered us out of the car, which was overheated and steaming. He wrestled with the back seat to get the tools. It was stuck and he kicked it. He took off his coat, rolled up his sleeves, and raised the left-hand side of the hood.

Dad seldom swore. An occasional "damn," perhaps, but he believed in setting a good example. Usually he stuck to such phrases as "by jingo" and "holy Moses." He said them both now, only there was something frightening in the way he rolled them out.

His head and shoulders disappeared into the inside of the hood. You could see his shirt, wet through, sticking to his back.

Nobody noticed Bill. He had crawled into the front seat. And then—"Kadookah. Kadookah."

Dad jumped so high he actually toppled into the engine, leaving his feet dangling in mid-air. His head butted the top of the hood and his right wrist came up against the red-hot exhaust pipe. You could hear the flesh sizzle. Finally he managed to extricate himself. He rubbed his head, and left grease across his forehead. He blew on the burned wrist. He was livid.

"Jesus Christ," he screamed, as if he had been saving this oath since his wedding day for just such an occasion. "Holy Jesus Christ. Who did that?"

"Mercy, Maud," said Mother, which was the closest she ever came to swearing, too.

Bill, who was six and always in trouble anyway, was the only one with nerve enough to laugh. But it was a nervous laugh at that.

"Did you see the birdie, Daddy?" he asked.

Dad grabbed him, and Bill stopped laughing.

"That was a good joke on you, Daddy," Bill said hopefully. But there wasn't much confidence in his voice.

"There is a time," Dad said through his teeth, "and there is a place for birdies. And there is a time and place for spankings."

"I'll bet you jumped six and nine-tenths inches, Daddy," said Bill, stalling for time, now.

Dad relaxed and let him go. "Yes, Billy, by jingo," he said. "That was a good joke on me, and I suspect I did jump six and nine-tenths inches."

Dad loved a joke on himself, all right. But he loved it best a few months after the joke was over, and not when it was happening. The story about Bill and the birdie became one of his favorites. No one ever laughed harder at the end of the story than Dad. Unless it was Bill. By jingo.

CHAPTER 3

Orphans in Uniform

WHEN Dad decided he wanted to take the family for an outing in the Pierce Arrow, he'd whistle assembly, and then ask:

"How many want to go for a ride?"

The question was purely rhetorical, for when Dad rode, everybody rode. So we'd all say we thought a ride would be fine.

Actually, this would be pretty close to the truth. Although Dad's driving was fraught with peril, there was a strange fascination in its brushes with death and its dramatic, traffic-stopping scenes. It was the sort of thing that you wouldn't have initiated yourself, but wouldn't have wanted to miss. It was standing up in a roller coaster. It was going up on the stage when the magician called for volunteers. It was a back somersault off the high diving board.

A drive, too, meant a chance to be with Dad and Mother. If you were lucky, even to sit with them on the front seat. There were so many of us and so few of them that we never could see as much of them as we wanted. Every hour or so, we'd change places so as to give someone else a turn in the front seat with them.

Dad would tell us to get ready while he brought the car around to the front of the house. He made it sound easy—as if it never entered his head that Foolish Carriage might not *want* to come around front. Dad was a perpetual optimist, confident that brains someday would triumph over inanimate steel; bolstered in the belief that he entered the fray with clean hands and a pure heart.

While groans, fiendish gurglings and backfires were emitting from the barn, the house itself would be organized confusion, as the family carried out its preparations in accordance with prearranged plans. It was like a newspaper on election night; general staff headquarters on D-Day minus one.

Getting ready meant scrubbed hands and face, shined shoes, clean clothes, combed hair. It wasn't advisable to be late, if and when Dad finally came rolling up to the porte-cochere. And it wasn't advisable to be dirty, because he'd inspect us all.

Besides getting himself ready, each older child was responsible for one of the younger ones. Anne was in charge of Dan, Ern in charge of Jack, and Mart in charge of Bob. This applied not only to rides in the car but all the time. The older sister was supposed to help her particular charge get dressed in the morning, to see that he made his bed, to put clean clothes on when he needed them, to see that he was washed and on time for meals, and to see that his process charts were duly initialed.

Anne, as the oldest, also was responsible for the deportment and general appearance of the whole group. Mother, of course, watched out for the baby, Jane. The intermediate children, Frank, Bill, Lill and Fred, were considered old enough to look out for themselves, but not old enough to look after anyone else. Dad, for the purpose of convenience (his own), ranked himself with the intermediate category.

In the last analysis, the person responsible for making the system work was Mother. Mother never threatened, never shouted or became excited, never spanked a single one of her children—or anyone else's, either.

Mother was a psychologist. In her own way, she got even better results with the family than Dad. But she was not a disciplinarian. If it was always Dad, and never Mother, who suggested going for a ride, Mother had her reasons.

She'd go from room to room, settling fights, drying tears, buttoning jackets.

"Mother, he's got my shirt. *Make* him give it to me."

"Mother, can I sit up front with you? I *never* get to sit up front."

"It's mine; you gave it to me. You wore mine yesterday."

When we'd all gathered in front of the house, the girls in dusters, the boys in linen suits, Mother would call the roll. Anne, Ernestine, Martha, Frank and so forth.

We used to claim that the roll-call was a waste of time and motion. Nothing was considered more of a sin in our house than wasted time and motions. But Dad had two vivid memories about children who had been left behind by mistake.

One such occurrence happened in Hoboken, aboard the liner *Leviathan*. Dad had taken the boys aboard on a sightseeing trip just before she sailed. He hadn't remembered to count noses when he came down the gangplank, and didn't notice, until the gangplank was pulled in, that Dan was missing. The *Leviathan's* sailing was held up for twenty minutes until Dan was located, asleep in a chair on the promenade deck.

The other occurrence was slightly more lurid. We were en route from Montclair to New Bedford, Massachusetts, and Frank, Jr., was left behind by mistake in a restaurant in New London. His absence wasn't discovered until near the end of the trip.

Dad wheeled the car around frantically and sped back to New London, breaking every traffic rule then on the books. We had stopped in the New London restaurant for lunch, and it had seemed a respectable enough place. It was night time when we returned, however, and the place was garish in colored lights. Dad left us in the car, and entered. After the drive in the dark, his eyes were squinted in the bright lights, and he couldn't see very well. But he hurried back to the booths and peered into each one.

A pretty young lady, looking for business, was drinking a highball in the second booth. Dad peered in, flustered.

"Hello, Pops," she said. "Don't be bashful. Are you looking for a naughty little girl?"

Dad was caught off guard.

"Goodness, no," he stammered, with all of his ordinary poise shattered. "I'm looking for a naughty little boy."

"Whoops, dearie," she said. "Pardon *me*."

All of us had been instructed that when we were lost we were supposed to stay in the same spot until someone returned for us, and Frank, Jr., was found, eating ice cream with the proprietor's daughter, back in the kitchen.

Anyway, those two experiences explain why Dad always insisted that the roll be called.

As we'd line up in front of the house before getting into the car, Dad would look us all over carefully.

"Are you all reasonably sanitary?" he would ask.

Dad would get out and help Mother and the two babies into

the front seat. He'd pick out someone whose behavior had been especially good, and allow him to sit up front too, as the left-hand lookout. The rest of us would pile in the back, exchanging kicks and pinches under the protection of the lap robe as we squirmed around trying to make more room.

Finally, off we'd start. Mother, holding the two babies, seemed to glow with vitality. Her red hair, arranged in a flat pompadour, would begin to blow out in wisps from her hat. As long as we were still in town, and Dad wasn't driving fast, she seemed to enjoy the ride. She'd sit there listening to him and carrying on a rapid conversation. But just the same her ears were straining toward the sounds in the back seats, to make sure that everything was going all right.

She had plenty to worry about, too, because the more cramped we became the more noise we'd make. Finally, even Dad couldn't stand the confusion.

"What's the matter back there?" he'd bellow to Anne. "I thought I told you to keep everybody quiet."

"That would require an act of God," Anne would reply bitterly.

"You are going to think God is acting if you don't keep order back there. I said quiet and I want quiet."

"I'm trying to make them behave, Daddy. But no one will listen to me."

"I don't want any excuses; I want order. You're the oldest. From now on, I don't want to hear a single sound from back there. Do you all want to walk home?"

By this time, most of us did, but no one dared say so.

Things would quiet down for a while. Even Anne would relax and forget her responsibilities as the oldest. But finally there'd be trouble again, and we'd feel pinches and kicks down underneath the robe.

"Cut it out, Ernestine, you sneak," Anne would hiss.

"You take up all the room," Ernestine would reply. "Why don't you move over. I wish you'd stayed home."

"You don't wish it half as much as I," Anne would say, with all her heart. It was on such occasions that Anne wished she were an only child.

We made quite a sight rolling along in the car, with the top down. As we passed through cities and villages, we caused a stir equaled only by a circus parade.

This was the part Dad liked best of all. He'd slow down to five miles an hour and he'd blow the horns at imaginary obstacles and cars two blocks away. The horns were Dad's calliope.

"I seen eleven of them, not counting the man and the woman," someone would shout from the sidewalk.

"You missed the second baby up front here, Mister," Dad would call over his shoulder.

Mother would make believe she hadn't heard anything, and look straight ahead.

Pedestrians would come scrambling from side streets and children would ask their parents to lift them onto their shoulders.

"How do you grow them carrot-tops, Brother?"

"These?" Dad would bellow. "These aren't so much, Friend. You ought to see the ones I left at home."

Whenever the crowds gathered at some intersection where we were stopped by traffic, the inevitable question came sooner or later.

"How do you feed all those kids, Mister?"

Dad would ponder for a minute. Then, rearing back so those on the outskirts could hear, he'd say as if he had just thought it up:

"Well, they come cheaper by the dozen, you know."

This was designed to bring down the house, and usually it did. Dad had a good sense of theater, and he'd try to time this apparent ad lib so that it would coincide with the change in traffic. While the peasantry was chuckling, the Pierce Arrow would buck away in clouds of gray smoke, while the professor up front rendered a few bars of Honk Honk Kadookah.

Leave 'em in stitches, that was us.

Dad would use that same "cheaper by the dozen" line whenever we stopped at a toll gate, or went to a movie, or bought tickets for a train or boat.

"Do my Irishmen come cheaper by the dozen?" he'd ask the man at the toll bridge. Dad could take one look at a man and know his nationality.

"Irishmen is it? And I might have known it. Lord love you, and it takes the Irish to raise a crew of red-headed Irishmen like that. The Lord Jesus didn't mean for any family like that to pay toll on my road. Drive through on the house."

"If he knew you were a Scot he'd take a shillalah and wrap it around your tight-fisted head," Mother giggled as we drove on.

"He probably would," Dad agreed. "Bejabers."

And one day at the circus.

"Do my Dutchmen come cheaper by the dozen?"

"Dutchmen? Ach. And what a fine lot of healthy Dutchmen."

"Have you heard the story about the man with the big family who took his children to the circus?" asked Dad. " 'My kids want to see your elephants,' said the man. 'That's nothing,' replied the ticket-taker, 'my elephants want to see your kids.' "

"I heard it before," said the circus man. "Often. Just go in that gate over there where there ain't no turnstile."

Mother only drew the line once at Dad's scenes in Foolish Carriage. That was in Hartford, Connecticut, right in the center of town. We had just stopped at a traffic sign, and the usual crowd was beginning to collect. We heard the words plainly from a plump lady near the curb.

"Just look at those poor, adorable little children," she said. "Don't they look sweet in their uniforms?"

Dad was all set to go into a new act—the benevolent superintendent taking the little orphan tykes out for a drive.

"Why bless my soul and body," he began loudly, in a jovial voice. "Why bless my buttons. Why bless . . ."

But for once Mother exploded.

"That," she said, "is the last straw. Positively and emphatically the ultimate straw."

This was something new, and Dad was scared. "What's the matter, Lillie?" he asked quickly.

"Not the penultimate, nor yet the ante-penultimate," said Mother. "But the ultimate."

"What's the matter, Lillie? Speak to me, girl."

"The camel's back is broken," Mother said. "Someone has just mistaken us for an orphanage."

"Oh, that," said Dad. "Sure, I know it. Wasn't it a scream?"

"No," said Mother. "It wasn't."

"It's these dusters we have to wear," Anne almost wept. "It's these damned, damned dusters. They look just like uniforms."

"Honestly, Daddy," said Ernestine, "it's so embarrassing to go riding when you always make these awful scenes."

The crowd was bigger than ever now.

"I," said Martha, "feel like Lady Godiva."

Mother was upset, but not too upset to reprimand Anne for swearing. Dad started to shake with laughter, and the crowd started laughing, too.

"That's a good one," somebody shouted. "Lady Godiva. You tell him, Sis. Lady Godiva!"

The boys began showing off. Bill sat on the top of the back seat as if he were a returning hero being cheered by a welcoming populace. He waved his hat aloft and bowed graciously to either side, with a fixed, stagey smile on his face. Frank and Fred swept imaginary ticker tape off his head and shoulders. But the girls, crimson-faced, dived under the lap robe.

"Get down from there, Bill," said Mother.

Dad was still roaring. "I just don't understand you girls," he wheezed. "That's the funniest thing I ever heard in my life. An orphanage on wheels. And me the superintendent. Gilbreth's Retreat for the Red-Haired Offspring of Unwed but Repentant Reprobates."

"Not humorous," said Mother. "Let's get out of here."

As we passed through the outskirts of Hartford, Dad was subdued and repentant; perhaps a little frightened.

"I didn't mean any harm, Lillie," he said.

"Of course you didn't, dear. And there's no harm done."

But Ernestine wasn't one to let an advantage drop.

"Well, we're through with the dusters," she announced from the back seat. "We'll never wear them again. Never again. Quoth the raven, and I quoth, 'Nevermore,' and I unquoth."

Dad could take it from Mother, but not from his daughters.

"Who says you're through with the dusters?" he howled. "Those dusters cost a lot of money, which does not grow on grape arbors. And if you think for a minute that . . ."

"No, Frank," Mother interrupted. "This time the girls are right. No more dusters."

It was a rare thing for them to disagree, and we all sat there enjoying it.

"All right, Lillie," Dad grinned, and everything was all right now. "As I always say, you're the boss. And I unquoth, too."

CHAPTER 4

Visiting Mrs. Murphy

ROADS weren't marked very well in those days, and Dad never believed in signs anyway.

"Probably some kid has changed those arrows around," he would say, possibly remembering his own youth. "Seems to me that if we turned that way, the way the arrow says, we'd be headed right back where we came from."

The same thing happened with the Automobile Blue Book, the tourist's bible in the early days of the automobile. Mother would read to him:

"Six-tenths of a mile past windmill, bear left at brick church and follow paved road."

"That must be the wrong windmill," Dad would say. "No telling when the fellow who wrote that book came over this road to check up on things. My bump of direction tells me to

27

turn right. They must have torn down the windmill the book's talking about."

Then, after he'd turned right and gotten lost, he'd blame Mother for giving him the wrong directions. Several times, he called Anne up to the front seat to read the Blue Book for him.

"Your Mother hasn't a very good sense of direction," he'd say loudly, glaring over his pince-nez at Mother. "She tells me to turn left when the book says to turn right. Then she blames me when we get lost. Now you read it to me just like it says. Don't change a single word, understand? And don't be making up anything about windmills that aren't there, or non-existent brick churches, just to confuse me. Read it just like it says."

But he wouldn't follow Anne's directions, either, and so he'd get lost just the same.

When things looked hopeless, Dad would ask directions at a store or filling station. He'd listen, and then usually drive off in exactly the opposite direction from the one his informant had indicated.

"Old fool," Dad would mutter. "He's lived five miles from Trenton all his life and he doesn't even know how to get there. He's trying to route me back to New York."

Mother was philosophical about it. Whenever she considered that Dad was hopelessly lost, she'd open a little portable ice box that she kept on the floor of the car under her feet, and hand Jane her bottle. This was Mother's signal that it was time to have lunch.

"All right, Lillie," Dad would say. "Guess we might as well stop and eat, while I get my bearings. You pick out a good place for a picnic."

While we were eating, Dad would keep looking around for

something that might be interesting. He was a natural teacher, and believed in utilizing every minute. Eating, he said, was "unavoidable delay." So were dressing, face-washing, and hair-combing. "Unavoidable delay" was not to be wasted.

If Dad found an ant hill, he'd tell us about certain colonies of ants that kept slaves and herds of cows. Then we'd take turns lying on our stomachs, watching the ants go back and forth picking up crumbs from sandwiches.

"See, they all work and they don't waste anything," Dad would say, and you could tell that the ant was one of his favorite creatures. "Look at the teamwork, as four of them try to move that piece of meat. That's motion study for you."

Or he'd point out a stone wall and say it was a perfect example of engineering. He'd explain about how the glaciers passed over the earth many years ago, and left the stone when they melted.

If a factory was nearby, he'd explain how you used a plumb line to get the chimney straight and why the windows had been placed a certain way to let in the maximum light. If the factory whistle blew, he'd take out his stopwatch and time the difference between when the steam appeared and when we heard the sound.

"Now take out your notebooks and pencils and I'll show you how to figure the speed of sound," he'd say.

He insisted that we make a habit of using our eyes and ears every single minute.

"Look there," he'd say. "What do you see? Yes, I know, it's a tree. But look at it. Study it. What do you *see?*"

But it was Mother who spun the stories that made the things we studied really unforgettable. If Dad saw motion study and team-work in an ant hill, Mother saw a highly complex civilization governed, perhaps, by a fat old queen who had a thousand black slaves bring her breakfast in bed mornings. If Dad stopped to explain the construction of a bridge, she would find the workman in his blue jeans, eating his lunch high on the top of the span. It was she who made us feel the breathless height of the structure and the relative puniness of the humans who had built it. Or if Dad pointed out a tree that had been bent and gnarled, it was Mother who made us sense how the wind, beating against the tree in the endless passing of time, had made its own relentless mark.

We'd sit there memorizing every word, and Dad would look at Mother as if he was sure he had married the most wonderful person in the world.

Before we left our picnic site, Dad would insist that all of the sandwich wrappings and other trash be carefully gathered, stowed in the lunch box, and brought home for disposal.

"If there's anything I can't stand, it's a sloppy camper," he'd say. "We don't want to leave a single scrap of paper on this man's property. We're going to leave things just like we found them, only even more so. We don't want to overlook so much as an apple peel."

Apple peels were a particularly sore subject. Most of us liked our apples without skins, and Dad thought this was wasteful. When he ate an apple, he consumed skin, core and seeds, which he alleged were the most healthful and most delectable portions of the fruit. Instead of starting at the side and eating his way around the equator, Dad started at the North Pole, and ate down through the core to the South.

He didn't actually forbid us to peel our apples or waste the cores, but he kept referring to the matter so as to let us know that he had noticed what we were doing.

Sometimes, in order to make sure that we left no rubbish behind, he'd have us form a line, like a company front in the army, and march across the picnic ground. Each of us was expected to pick up any trash in the territory that he covered.

The result was that we often came home with the leavings of countless previous picnickers.

"I don't see how you children can possibly clutter up a place the way you do," Dad would grin as he stuffed old papers, bottles, and rusty tin cans into the picnic box.

"That's not our mess, Daddy. You know that just as well as we do. What would we be doing with empty whiskey bottles and a last year's copy of the Hartford *Courant?*"

"That's what I'd like to know," he'd say, while sniffing the bottles.

Neither Dad nor Mother thought filling station toilets were sanitary. They never elaborated about just what diseases the toilets contained, but they made it plain that the ailments were both contagious and dire. In comparison, leprosy would be no worse than a bad cold. Dad always opened the door of a public rest room with his coattail, and the preparations and precautions that ensued were "unavoidable delay" in its worst aspect.

Once he and Mother had discarded filling stations as a possibility, the only alternative was the woods. Perhaps it was the nervous strain of enduring Dad's driving; perhaps it was simply that fourteen persons have different personal habits. At any rate, we seemed to stop at every promising clump of trees.

"I've seen dogs that paid less attention to trees," Dad used to groan.

For family delicacy, Dad coined two synonyms for going to the bathroom in the woods. One was "visiting Mrs. Murphy." The other was "examining the rear tire." They meant the same thing.

After a picnic, he'd say:

"How many have to visit Mrs. Murphy?"

Usually nobody would. But after we had been under way ten or fifteen minutes, someone would announce that he had to go. So Dad would stop the car, and Mother would take the girls into the woods on one side of the road, while Dad took the boys into the woods on the other.

"I know every piece of flora and fauna from Bangor, Maine, to Washington, D.C.," Dad exclaimed bitterly.

On the way home, when it was dark, Bill used to crawl up into a swivel seat right behind Dad. Every time Dad was intent on steering while rounding a curve, Bill would reach forward and clutch his arm. Bill was a perfect mimic, and he'd whisper in Mother's voice, "Not so fast, Frank. Not so fast." Dad would think it was Mother grabbing his arm and whispering to him, and he'd make believe he didn't hear her.

Sometimes Bill would go into the act when the car was creeping along at a dignified thirty, and Dad finally would turn to Mother disgustedly and say:

"For the love of Mike, Lillie! I was only doing twenty."

He automatically subtracted ten miles an hour from the speed whenever he discussed the matter with Mother.

"I didn't say anything, Frank," Mother would tell him.

Dad would turn around, then, and see all of us giggling into our handkerchiefs. He'd give Bill a playful cuff and rumple his hair. Secretly, Dad was proud of Bill's imitations. He used to say that when Bill imitated a bird he (Dad) didn't dare to look up.

"You'll be the death of me yet, boy," Dad would say to Bill.

As we'd roll along, we'd sing three-and-four part harmony, with Mother and Dad joining in as soprano and bass. "Bobolink Swinging on the Bow," "Love's Old Sweet Song," "Our Highland Goat," "I've Been Working on the Railroad."

"What do only children *do* with themselves?" we'd think.

Dad would lean back against the seat and cock his hat on the side of his head. Mother would snuggle up against him as if she were cold. The babies were asleep now. Sometimes Mother turned around between songs and said to us: "Right now is the happiest time in the world." And perhaps it was.

CHAPTER 5

Mister Chairman

DAD was born in Fairfield, Maine, where his father ran a general store, farmed, and raised harness-racing horses. John Hiram Gilbreth died in 1871, leaving his three-year-old son, two older daughters, and a stern and rockbound widow.

Dad's mother, Grandma Gilbreth, believed that her children were fated to make important marks in the world, and that her first responsibility was to educate them so they would be prepared for their rendezvous with destiny.

"After that," she told her Fairfield neighbors, with a knowing nod, "blood will tell."

Without any business ties to hold her in Maine, she moved to Andover, Massachusetts, so that the girls could attend Abbott Academy. Later, when her oldest daughter showed a talent for music, Grandma Gilbreth decided to move again. Every New

Englander knew the location of the universe's seat of culture, and it was to Boston that she now journeyed with her flock.

Dad wanted, more than anything else, to be a construction engineer, and his mother planned to have him enter Massachusetts Institute of Technology. By the time he finished high school, though, he decided this would be too great a drain on the family finances, and would interfere with his sisters' studies. Without consulting his mother, he took a job as a bricklayer's helper.

Once the deed was done, Grandma Gilbreth decided to make the best of it. After all, Mr. Lincoln had started by splitting rails.

"But if you're going to be a bricklayer's helper," she said, "for mercy sakes be a good bricklayer's helper."

"I'll do my best to find a good bricklayer to help," Dad grinned.

If Grandma thought Dad was going to be a good helper, his new foreman thought he was the worst he had encountered in forty years, man and boy, of bricklaying.

During Dad's first week at work he made so many suggestions about how brick could be laid faster and better that the foreman threatened repeatedly to fire him.

"You're the one who came here to learn," the foreman hollered at him. "For Christ's sake don't try to learn us."

Subtle innuendoes like that never worried Dad. Besides, he already knew that motion study was his element, and he had discovered something that apparently had never attracted the attention of industry before. He tried to explain it to the foreman.

"Did you ever notice that no two men use exactly the same way of laying bricks?" he asked. "That's important, and do you know why?"

"I know that if you open your mouth about bricklaying again, I'll lay a brick in it."

"It's important because if one bricklayer is doing the job the right way, then all the others are doing the job the wrong way. Now if I had your job, I'd find who's laying brick the right way, and make all the others copy him."

"If you had my job," shouted the livid-faced foreman, "the first thing you'd do is fire the red-headed unprintable son of a ruptured deleted who tried to get *your* job. And that's what I think you're trying to do."

He picked up a brick and waved it menacingly.

"I may not be smart enough to know who my best bricklayer is, but I know who my worst hod-carrier is. I'm warning you, stop bothering me or this brick goes in your mouth—edgewise."

Within a year, Dad designed a scaffold that made him the fastest bricklayer on the job. The principle of the scaffold was that loose bricks and mortar always were at the level of the top of the wall being built. The other bricklayers had to lean over to get their materials. Dad didn't.

"You ain't smart," the foreman scoffed. "You're just too God-damned lazy to squat."

But the foreman had identical scaffolds built for all the men on the job, and even suggested that Dad send the original to the Mechanics Institute, where it won a prize. Later, on the foreman's recommendation, Dad was made foreman of a crew of his own. He achieved such astonishing speed records that he was promoted to superintendent, and then went into the contracting business for himself, building bridges, canals, industrial towns, and factories. Sometimes, after the contract work was finished, he was asked to remain on the job to install his motion study methods within the factory itself.

By the time he was twenty-seven, he had offices in New York,

Boston, and London. He had a yacht, smoked cigars, and had a reputation as a snappy dresser.

Mother came from a well-to-do family in Oakland, California. She had met Dad in Boston while she was en route to Europe on one of those well-chaperoned tours for fashionable young ladies of the 'nineties.

Mother was a Phi Beta Kappa and a psychology graduate of the University of California. In those days women who were scholars were viewed with some suspicion. When Mother and Dad were married, the Oakland paper said:

"Although a graduate of the University of California, the bride is nonetheless an extremely attractive young woman."

Indeed she was.

So it was Mother the psychologist and Dad the motion study man and general contractor, who decided to look into the new field of the psychology of management, and the old field of psychologically managing a houseful of children. They believed that what would work in the home would work in the factory, and what would work in the factory would work in the home.

Dad put the theory to a test shortly after we moved to Montclair. The house was too big for Tom Grieves, the handyman, and Mrs. Cunningham, the cook, to keep in order. Dad decided we were going to have to help them, and he wanted us to offer the help of our own accord. He had found that the best way to get cooperation out of employees in a factory was to set up a joint employer-employee board, which would make work assignments on a basis of personal choice and aptitude. He and Mother set up a Family Council, patterned after an employer-employee board. The council met every Sunday afternoon, immediately after dinner.

At the first session, Dad got to his feet formally, poured a glass of ice water, and began a speech.

"You will notice," he said, "that I am installed here as your chairman. I assume there are no objections. The chair, hearing no objections, will . . ."

"Mr. Chairman," Anne interrupted. Being in high school, she knew something of parliamentary procedure, and thought it might be a good idea to have the chairman represent the common people.

"Out of order," said Dad. "Very much out of order when the chair has the floor."

"But you said you heard no objections, and I want to object."

"Out of order means sit down, and you're out of order," Dad shouted. He took a swallow of ice water, and resumed his speech. "The first job of the Council is to apportion necessary work in the house and yard. Does the chair hear any suggestions?"

There were no suggestions. Dad forced a smile and attempted to radiate good humor.

"Come, come, fellow members of the Council," he said. "This is a democracy. Everybody has an equal voice. How do you want to divide the work?"

No one wanted to divide the work or otherwise be associated with it in any way, shape, or form. No one said anything.

"In a democracy everybody speaks," said Dad, "so, by jingo, start speaking." The Good Humor Man was gone now. "Jack, I recognize you. What do you think about dividing the work? I warn you, you'd better think something."

"I think," Jack said slowly, "that Mrs. Cunningham and Tom should do the work. They get paid for it."

"Sit down," Dad hollered. "You are no longer recognized."

Jack sat down amid general approval, except that of Dad and Mother.

"Hush, Jackie," Mother whispered. "They may hear you and leave. It's so hard to get servants when there are so many children in the house."

"I wish they would leave," said Jack. "They're too bossy."

Dan was next recognized by the chair.

"I think Tom and Mrs. Cunningham have enough to do," he said, as Dad and Mother beamed and nodded agreement. "I think we should hire more people to work for us."

"Out of order," Dad shouted. "Sit down and be quiet!"

Dad saw things weren't going right. Mother was the psychologist. Let her work them out.

"Your chairman recognizes the assistant chairman," he said, nodding to Mother to let her know he had just conferred that title upon her person.

"We could hire additional help," Mother said, "and that might be the answer."

We grinned and nudged each other.

"But," she continued, "that would mean cutting the budget somewhere else. If we cut out all desserts and allowances, we could afford a maid. And if we cut out moving pictures, ice cream sodas, and new clothes for a whole year, we could afford a gardener, too."

"Do I hear a motion to that effect?" Dad beamed. "Does anybody want to stop allowances?"

No one did. After some prodding by Dad, the motion on allotting work finally was introduced and passed. The boys would cut the grass and rake the leaves. The girls would sweep, dust and do the supper dishes. Everyone except Dad would make his own bed and keep his room neat. When it came to apportioning work on an aptitude basis, the smaller girls were assigned to dust the legs and lower shelves of furniture; the older girls to dust table tops and upper shelves. The older boys would push the lawnmowers and carry leaves. The younger ones would do the raking and weeding.

The next Sunday, when Dad convened the second meeting of the Council, we sat self-consciously around the table, biding our time. The chairman knew something was in the air, and it tickled him. He had trouble keeping a straight face when he called for new business.

Martha, who had been carefully coached in private caucus, arose.

"It has come to the attention of the membership," she began, "that the assistant chairman intends to buy a new rug for the dining room. Since the entire membership will be required to look upon, and sit in chairs resting upon, the rug, I move that the Council be consulted before any rug is purchased."

"Second the motion," said Anne.

Dad didn't know what to make of this one. "Any discussion?" he asked, in a move designed to kill time while he planned his counter attack.

"Mr. Chairman," said Lillian. "We have to sweep it. We should be able to choose it."

"We want one with flowers on it," Martha put in. "When you have flowers, the crumbs don't show so easily, and you save motions by not having to sweep so often."

"We want to know what sort of a rug the assistant chairman intends to buy," said Ernestine.

"We want to make sure the budget can afford it," Fred announced.

"I recognize the assistant chairman," said Dad. "This whole Council business was your idea anyway, Lillie. What do we do now?"

"Well," Mother said doubtfully, "I had planned to get a plain violet-colored rug, and I had planned to spend a hundred dollars. But if the children think that's too much, and if they want flowers, I'm willing to let the majority rule."

"I move," said Frank, "that not more than ninety-five dollars be spent."

Dad shrugged his shoulders. If Mother didn't care, he certainly didn't.

"So many as favor the motion to spend only ninety-five dollars, signify by saying aye."

The motion carried unanimously.

"Any more new business?"

"I move," said Bill, "that we spend the five dollars we have saved to buy a collie puppy."

"Hey, wait a minute," said Dad. The rug had been somewhat of a joke, but the dog question was serious. We had wanted a dog for years. Dad thought that any pet which didn't lay eggs was an extravagance that a man with twelve children could ill afford. He felt that if he surrendered on the dog question, there was no telling what the Council might vote next. He had a sickening mental picture of a barn full of ponies, a roadster for Anne, motorcycles, a swimming pool, and, ultimately, the poor house or a debtors' prison, if they still had such things.

"Second the motion," said Lillian, yanking Dad out of his reverie.

"A dog," said Jack, "would be a pet. Everyone in the family could pat him, and I would be his master."

"A dog," said Dan, "would be a friend. He could eat scraps of food. He would save us waste and would save motions for the garbage man."

"A dog," said Fred, "would keep burglars away. He would sleep on the foot of my bed, and I would wash him whenever he was dirty."

"A dog," Dad mimicked, "would be an accursed nuisance. He would be our master. He would eat me out of house and home. He would spread fleas from the garret to the porte-cochere. He would be positive to sleep on the foot of *my* bed. Nobody would wash his filthy, dirty, flea-bitten carcass."

He looked pleadingly at Mother.

"Lillie, Lillie, open your eyes," he implored. "Don't you see where this is leading us? Ponies, roadsters, trips to Hawaii, silk stockings, rouge, and bobbed hair."

"I think, dear," said Mother, "that we must rely on the good sense of the children. A five-dollar dog is not a trip to Hawaii."

We voted, and there was only one negative ballot—Dad's. Mother abstained. In after years, as the collie grew older, shed hair on the furniture, bit the mailman, and did in fact try to appropriate the foot of Dad's bed, the chairman was heard to remark on occasion to the assistant chairman:

"I give nightly praise to my Maker that I never cast a ballot to bring that lazy, disreputable, ill-tempered beast into what was once my home. I'm glad I had the courage to go on record as opposing that illegitimate, shameless flea-bag that now shares my bed and board. You abstainer, you!"

CHAPTER 6

Touch System

LIKE most of Dad's and Mother's ideas, the Family Council was basically sound and, although it verged sometimes on the hysterical, brought results. Family purchasing committees, duly elected, bought the food, clothes, furniture, and athletic equipment. A utilities committee levied one-cent fines on wasters of water and electricity. A projects committee saw that work was completed as scheduled. Allowances were decided by the Council, which also meted out rewards and punishment. Despite Dad's forebodings, there were no ponies or roadsters.

One purchasing committee found a large department store which gave us wholesale rates on everything from underwear to baseball gloves. Another bought canned goods directly from a manufacturer, in truckload lots.

It was the Council, too, which worked out the system of submitting bids for unusual jobs to be done.

When Lill was eight, she submitted a bid of forty-seven cents to paint a long, high fence in the back yard. Of course it was the lowest bid, and she got the job.

"She's too young to try to paint that fence all by herself," Mother told Dad. "Don't let her do it."

"Nonsense," said Dad. "She's got to learn the value of money and to keep agreements. Let her alone."

Lill, who was saving for a pair of roller skates and wanted the money, kept insisting she could do it.

"If you start it, you'll have to finish it," Dad said.

"I'll finish it, Daddy. I know I can."

"You've got yourself a contract, then."

It took Lill ten days to finish the job, working every day after school and all day week ends. Her hands blistered, and some nights she was so tired she couldn't sleep. It worried Dad so that some nights he didn't sleep very well either. But he made her live up to her contract.

"You've got to let her stop," Mother kept telling him. "She'll have a breakdown or something—or else you will."

"No," said Dad. "She's learning the value of money and she's learning that when you start something it's necessary to finish it if you want to collect. She's got to finish. It's in her contract."

"You sound like Shylock," Mother said.

But Dad stood firm.

When Lill finally completed the job, she came to Dad in tears.

"It's done," she said. "I hope you're satisfied. Now can I have my forty-seven cents?"

Dad counted out the change.

"Don't cry, honey," he said. "No matter what you think of your old Daddy, he did it for your own good. If you go look under your pillow you'll find that Daddy really loved you all the time."

The present was a pair of roller skates.

Fred headed the utilities committee and collected the fines. Once, just before he went to bed, he found that someone had left a faucet dripping and that there was a bathtub full of hot water. Jack had been asleep for more than an hour, but Fred woke him up.

"Get in there and take a bath," he said.

"But I had a bath just before I went to bed."

"I know you did, and you left the faucet dripping," Fred told him. "Do you want to waste that perfectly good water?"

"Why don't you take a bath?" Jack asked.

"I take my baths in the morning. You know that. That's the schedule."

Jack had two baths that night.

One day Dad came home with two victrolas and two stacks of records. He whistled assembly as he hit the front steps, and we helped him unload.

"Kids," he said, "I have a wonderful surprise. Two victrolas and all these lovely records."

"But we have a victrola, Daddy."

"I know that, but the victrola we have is the downstairs victrola. Now we are going to have two upstairs victrolas. Won't that be fun?"

"Why?"

"Well from now on," said Dad, "we are going to try to do away with unavoidable delay. The victrolas will go in the bathrooms—one in the boys' bathroom and the other in the girls' bathroom. I'll bet we'll be the only family in town with a victrola in every bath. And when you are taking a bath, or brushing your teeth, or otherwise occupied, you will play the victrolas."

"Why?"

"Why, why, why," mimicked Dad. "Why this and why that. Does there have to be a why for everything?"

"There doesn't have to be, Daddy," Ernestine explained patiently. "But with you there usually is. When you start talking about unavoidable delay and victrolas, dance music is not the first thing that pops into our minds."

"No," Dad admitted. "It's not dance music. But you're going to find this is just as good in a way, and more educational."

"What kind of records are they?" Anne asked.

"Well," Dad said, "they are very entertaining. They are French and German language lesson records. You don't have to listen to them consciously. Just play them. And they'll finally make an impression."

"Oh, no!"

Dad soon tired of diplomacy and psychology.

"Shut up and listen to me," he roared. "I have spent one hundred and sixty dollars for this equipment. Did I get it for myself? I most emphatically by jingo well did not. I happen already to be able to speak German and French with such fluency that I frequently am mistaken for a native of both of those countries."

This was at best a terribly gross exaggeration, for while Dad had studied languages for most of his adult life, he never had become very familiar with French, although he could stumble along fairly well in German. Usually he insisted that Mother accompany him as an interpreter on his business trips to Europe. Languages came naturally to Mother.

"No," Dad continued, "I did not buy this expensive equipment for myself, although I must say I would like nothing better than to have my own private victrola and my own private language records. I bought it for you, as a present. And you are going to use it. If those two victrolas aren't going every morning from the minute you get up until you come down to breakfast, I'm going to know the reason why."

"One reason," said Bill, "might be that it is impossible to change records while you are in the bathtub."

"A person who applies motion study can be in and out of the tub in the time it takes one record to play."

That was perfectly true. Dad would sit in the tub and put the soap in his right hand. Then he'd place his right hand on his left shoulder and run it down the top of his left arm, back up the bottom of his left arm to his armpit, down his side, down the outside of his left leg, and then up the inside of his left leg. Then he'd change the soap to his left hand and do the same thing to his right side. After a couple of circular strokes on his midsection and his back, and some special attention to his feet and face, he'd duck under for a rinse and get out. He had all the boys in the bathroom several times to demonstrate just how he did it, and he sat in the middle of the living room rug one day, with all his clothes on, to teach the girls.

So there was no more unavoidable delay in the bathroom, and it wasn't long before we were all speaking at least a pidgin variety of French and German. For ten years, the victrolas ground out their lessons on the second floor of our Montclair house. As we became fairly fluent, we often would speak the languages at the dinner table. Dad was left out of the conversation when the talk was in French.

"Your German accents are not so bad," he said. "I can understand most of what you say when you talk German. But your French accents are so atrocious that no one but yourselves could possibly understand you. I believe you've developed some exotic language all your own, which has no more relation to French than it does to Pig Latin."

We giggled, and he turned furiously to Mother.

"Don't you think so, Lillie?"

"Well, dear," she said. "I don't think anyone would mistake them for natives of France, but I can usually make out what they're getting at."

"That," said Dad, with some dignity, "is because you learned your French in this country, where everybody talks with an accent, whereas my knowledge of the language came straight from the streets of Paris."

"Maybe so, dear," said Mother. "Maybe so."

That night, Dad moved the boys' bathroom victrola into his bedroom, and we heard him playing French records, far into the night.

At about the time that he brought home the victrolas, Dad became a consultant to the Remington typewriter company and, through motion study methods, helped Remington develop the world's fastest typist. /

He told us about it one night at dinner—how he had put little flashing lights on the fingers of the typist and taken moving pictures and time exposures to see just what motions she employed and how those motions could be reduced.

"Anyone can learn to type fast," Dad concluded. "Why I've got a system that will teach touch typing in two weeks. Absolutely guaranteed."

You could see the Great Experiment hatching in his mind.

"In two weeks," he repeated. "Why I could even teach a child to type touch system in two weeks."

"Can you type touch system, Daddy?" Bill asked.

"In two weeks," said Dad. "I could teach a child. Anybody can do it if he will do just exactly what I tell him to do."

The next day he brought home a new, perfectly white typewriter, a gold knife, and an Ingersoll watch. He unwrapped them and put them on the dining room table.

"Can I try the typewriter, Daddy?" asked Mart.

"Why is the typewriter white?" Anne wanted to know. "All typewriters I've ever seen were black. It's beautiful, all right, but why is it white?"

"It's white so that it will photograph better," Dad explained. "Also, for some reason, anyone who sees a white typewriter wants to type on it. Don't ask me why. It's psychology."

All of us wanted to use it, but Dad wouldn't let anyone touch it but himself.

"This is an optional experiment," he said. "I believe I can teach the touch system in two weeks. Anyone who wants to learn will be able to practice on the white machine. The one who can type the fastest at the end of two weeks will receive the typewriter as a present. The knife and watch will be prizes awarded on a handicap basis, taking age into consideration."

Except for the two youngest, who still weren't talking, we all said we wanted to learn.

"Can I practice first, Daddy?" Lill asked.

"No one practices until I say 'practice.' Now first I will show you how the typewriter works." Dad got a sheet of paper. "The paper goes in here. You turn this—so-oo. And you push the carriage over to the end of the line—like this."

And Dad, using two fingers, hesitatingly pecked out the first thing that came to his mind—his name.

"Is that the touch system, Daddy?" Bill asked.

"No," said Dad. "I'll show you the touch system in a little while."

"Do you know the touch system, Daddy?"

"Let's say I know how to teach it, Billy boy."

"But do you know it yourself, Daddy?"

"I know how to teach it," Dad shouted. "In two weeks, I can teach it to a child. Do you hear me? I have just finished helping to develop the fastest typist in the world. Do you hear that? They tell me Caruso's voice teacher can't sing a by jingoed note. Does that answer your question?"

"I guess so," said Bill.

"Any other questions?"

There weren't. Dad then brought out some paper diagrams of a typewriter keyboard, and passed one to each of us.

"The first thing you have to do is to memorize that keyboard. QWERTYUIOP. Those are the letters in the top line. Memorize them. Get to know them forward and backwards. Get to know them so you can say them with your eyes closed. Like this."

Dad closed his right eye, but kept his left open just a slit so that he could still read the chart.

"QWERTYUIOP. See what I mean? Get to know them in your sleep. That's the first step."

We looked crestfallen.

"I know. You want to try out that white typewriter. Pretty, isn't it?"

He clicked a few keys.

"Runs as smoothly as a watch, doesn't it?"

We said it did.

"Well, tomorrow or the next day you'll be using it. First you have to memorize the keyboard. Then you've got to learn what fingers to use. Then you'll graduate to Moby Dick here. And one of you will win him."

Once we had memorized the keyboard, our fingers were colored with chalk. The little fingers were colored blue, the index fingers red and so forth. Corresponding colors were placed on the key zones of the diagrams. For instance, the Q, A and Z, all of which are hit with the little finger of the left hand, were colored blue to match the blue little finger.

"All you have to do now is practice until each finger has learned the right color habit," Dad said. "And once you've got that, we'll be ready to start."

In two days we were fairly adept at matching the colors on our fingers with the colors on the keyboard diagrams. Ernestine was the fastest, and got the first chance to sit down at the white typewriter. She hitched her chair up to it confidently, while we all gathered around.

"Hey, no fair, Daddy," she wailed. "You've put blank caps on all the keys. I can't see what I'm typing."

Blank caps are fairly common now, but Dad had thought up the idea and had had them made specially by the Remington company.

"You don't have to see," Dad said. "Just imagine that those keys are colored, and type just like you were typing on the diagram."

Ern started slowly, and then picked up speed, as her fingers jumped instinctively from key to key. Dad stood in back of her, with a pencil in one hand and a diagram in the other. Every time she made a mistake, he brought the pencil down on the top of her head.

"Stop it Daddy. That hurts. I can't concentrate knowing that that pencil's about to descend on my head."

"It's meant to hurt. Your head has to teach your fingers not to make mistakes."

Ern typed along. About every fifth word, she'd make a mistake and the pencil would descend with a bong. But the bongs became less and less frequent and finally Dad put away the pencil.

"That's fine, Ernie," he said. "I believe I'll keep you."

By the end of the two weeks, all children over six years old and Mother knew the touch system reasonably well. Dad said he knew it, too. We were a long way from being fast—because nothing but practice gives speed—but we were reasonably accurate.

Dad entered Ernestine's name in a national speed contest, as a sort of child prodigy, but Mother talked him out of it and Ern never actually competed.

"It's not that I want to show her off," he told Mother. "It's just that I want to do the people a favor—to show them what can be done with proper instructional methods and motion study."

"I don't think it would be too good an idea, dear," Mother said. "Ernestine is high strung, and the children are conceited enough as it is."

Dad compromised by taking moving pictures of each of us, first with colored fingers practicing on the paper diagrams and then actually working on the typewriter. He said the pictures were "for my files," but about a month later they were released in a newsreel, which showed everything except the pencil descending on our heads. And some of us today recoil every time we touch the backspace key.

Since Dad thought eating was a form of unavoidable delay, he utilized the dinner hour as an instruction period. His primary rule was that no one could talk unless the subject was of general interest.

Dad was the one who decided what subjects were of general interest. Since he was convinced that everything he uttered was interesting, the rest of the family had trouble getting a word in edgewise.

"Honestly, we have the stupidest boy in our history class," Anne would begin.

"Is he cute?" Ernestine asked.

"Not of general interest," Dad roared.

"I'm interested," Mart said.

"But I," Dad announced, "am bored stiff. Now if Anne had seen a two-headed boy in history class, that would have been of general interest."

Usually at the start of a meal, while Mother served up the plates at one end of the table, Dad served up the day's topic of conversation at the other end.

"I met an engineer today who had just returned from India," he said. "What do you think he told me? He believes India has fewer industries for its size than has any other country in the world."

We knew, then, that for the duration of that particular meal even the dullest facts about India would be deemed of exceptional general interest; whereas neighboring Siam, Persia, China, and Mongolia would, for some reason, be considered of but slight general interest, and events which had transpired in Montclair, New Jersey, would be deemed of no interest whatsoever. Once India had been selected as the destination, Dad would head toward it as relentlessly as if Garcia were waiting there, and we had the message.

Sometimes, the topic of conversation was a motion study project, such as clearing off the dishes from the table. Motion study was always of great general interest.

"Is it better to stack the dishes on the table, so that you can carry out a big pile?" Dad asked. "Or is it better to take a few of them at a time into the butler's pantry, where you can rinse them while you stack? After dinner we'll divide the table into two parts, and try one method on one part and the other method on the other. I'll time you."

Also of exceptional general interest was a series of tricks whereby Dad could multiply large numbers in his head, without using pencil and paper. The explanation of how the tricks are worked is too complicated to explain in detail here, and two fairly elementary examples should suffice.

1. To multiply forty-six times forty-six, you figure how much greater forty-six is than twenty-five. The answer is twenty-one. Then you figure how much less forty-six is than fifty. The answer is four. You can square the four and get sixteen. You put the twenty-one and the sixteen together, and the answer is twenty-one sixteen, or 2,116.

2. To multiply forty-four times forty-four, you figure how much greater forty-four is than twenty-five. The answer is nineteen. Then you figure how much less forty-four is than fifty. The answer is six. You square the six and get thirty-six. You put the nineteen and the thirty-six together, and the answer is nineteen thirty-six, or 1,936.

"I want to teach all of you how to multiply two-digit numbers in your head," Dad announced at dinner.

"Not of general interest," said Anne.

"Now if you had learned to multiply a two-digit number by a two-headed calf," Ern suggested.

"Those who do not think it is of general interest may leave the table and go to their rooms," Dad said coldly, "and I understand there is apple pie for dessert."

Nobody left.

"Since everyone now appears to be interested," said Dad, "I will explain how it's done."

It was a complicated thing for children to understand, and it involved memorizing the squares of all numbers up to twenty-five. But Dad took it slowly, and within a couple of months the older children had learned all the tricks involved.

While Mother carved and served the plates—Dad sometimes carved wood for a hobby, but he never touched a carving knife at the table—Dad would shout out problems in mental arithmetic for us.

"Nineteen times seventeen."

"Three twenty-three."

"Right. Good boy, Bill."

"Fifty-two times fifty-two."

"Twenty-seven zero four."

"Right. Good girl, Martha."

Dan was five when this was going on, and Jack was three. One night at supper, Dad was firing questions at Dan on the squares of numbers up to twenty-five. This involved straight memory, and no mental arithmetic.

"Fifteen times fifteen," said Dad.

"Two twenty-five," said Dan.

"Sixteen times sixteen," said Dad.

Jack, sitting in his high chair next to Mother, gave the answer. "Two fifty-six."

At first Dad was irritated, because he thought one of the older children was butting in.

"I'm asking Dan," he said, "you older children stop showing off and . . ." Then he registered a double take.

"What did you say, Jackie boy?" Dad cooed.

"Two fifty-six."

Dad drew a nickel out of his pocket and grew very serious.

"Have you been memorizing the squares as I asked the questions to the older children, Jackie?"

Jack didn't know whether that was good or bad, but he nodded.

"If you can tell me what seventeen times seventeen is, Jackie boy, this nickel is yours."

"Sure, Daddy," said Jack. "Two eighty-nine."

Dad passed him the nickel and turned beaming to Mother. "Lillie," he said, "we'd better keep that boy, too."

Martha, at eleven, became the fastest in the family at mental mathematics. Still feeling frustrated because he hadn't been able to take Ernestine to the speed typing contest, Dad insisted on taking Martha to an adding machine exhibition in New York.

"No, Lillie," he told Mother. "This one is not high strung. I was willing to compromise on moving pictures of the typing, but you can't take movies of this. She goes to New York with me."

Martha stood up on a platform at the adding machine show, and answered the problems quicker than the calculators could operate. Dad, of course, stood along side her. After the final applause, he told the assemblage modestly:

"There's really nothing to it. I've got a boy named Jack at home who's almost as good as she is. I would have brought him here with me, but Mrs. Gilbreth said he's still too young. Maybe next year, when he's four . . ."

By this time, all of us had begun to suspect that Dad had his points as a teacher, and that he knew what he was talking about. There was one time, though, when he failed.

"Tomorrow," he told us at dinner, "I'm going to make a cement bird bath. All those who want to watch me should come home right after school, and we'll make it in the late afternoon."

Dad had long since given up general contracting, to devote all of his time to scientific management and motion study, but we knew he had been an expert bricklayer and had written a book on reinforced concrete.

The next afternoon he built a mold, mixed his concrete confidently, and poured his bird bath.

"We'll let it set for awhile, and then take the mold off," he said.

Dad had to go out of town for a few weeks. When he returned, he changed into old clothes, whistled assembly, and led us out into the yard.

"I've had this bird bath on my mind all the time I was away," he said. "It should be good and hard now."

"Will the birds come and take a bath in it, Daddy?" Fred asked.

"I would say, Freddy, that birds will come for miles to take a bath in it. Indeed, on Saturday nights I would say the birds will be standing in line to use our lovely bathtub."

He leaned over the mold. "Stand back, everybody," he said. "We will now unveil the masterpiece. Get your towels ready, little birdies, it's almost bathing time."

We stood hushed and waiting. But as he lifted the bird bath out of the mold, there was an unbelievable grating sound, and a pile of dust and rubble lay at our feet. Dad stood deflated and silent. He took it so seriously that we felt sorry for him.

"Never mind, Daddy," Lill said. "We know you tried, anyway."

"Bill," Dad said sternly. "Did you?"

"Did I what, Daddy?"

"Did you touch my bird bath?"

"No, Daddy, honest."

Dad reached down and picked up some of the concrete. It crumbled into dust between his fingers.

"Too much sand," he muttered. And then to Bill. "No, it's my fault. Too much sand. I know you didn't touch it, and I'm sorry I implied that you did."

But you couldn't keep Dad down for long.

"Well," he said, "that didn't work out so very well. But I've built some of the finest and tallest buildings in the whole world. And some bridges and roads and canals that stretch for miles and miles."

"Is a bird bath harder to build than a tall building, Daddy?" asked Dan.

Dad, deflated all over again, kicked the rubble with his toe and started toward the house.

"Too much sand," he muttered.

CHAPTER 7

Skipping Through School

MOTHER saw her children as a dozen individuals, a dozen different personalities, who eventually would have to make their ways separately in the world. Dad saw them as an all-inclusive group, to be brought up under one master plan that would be best for everybody. What was good for Anne, he believed, would be good for Ernestine, for Bill, for Jack.

Skipping grades in school was part of Dad's master plan. There was no need, he said, for his children to be held back by a school system geared for children of simply average parents.

Dad made periodic surprise visits to our schools to find out if and when we were ready to skip. Because of his home-training program—spelling games, geography quizzes, and the arithmetic and languages—we sometimes were prepared to skip; but never so prepared as Dad thought we should be.

The standard reward for skipping was a new bicycle. None of us used to like to jump grades, because it meant making new friends and trailing behind the rest of the class until we could make up the work. But the bicycle incentive was great, and there was always the fear that a younger brother or sister would skip and land in your class. That would be the disgrace supreme. So whenever it looked as if anyone down the family line was about to skip, every older child would study frantically so that he could jump ahead, too.

Mother saw the drawbacks. She knew that, while we were advanced for our age in some subjects, we were only average or below in some intangibles such as leadership and sociability. She knew, too, that Dad, who was in his fifties, wanted to get as many of his dozen as possible through school and college before he died.

As for report cards, members of the family who brought home good grades were feted and rewarded.

"Chip off the old block," Dad would crow. "Youngest in his class, and he brings home all A's. I used to lead my class in the fifth grade, too, and I was always the one picked to draw the turkey on the blackboard come Thanksgiving. My only bad subject was spelling. Never learned to spell until I was a grown man. I used to tell the teachers that I'd be able to hire a bunch of stenographers to do my spelling for me."

Then he'd lean back and roar. You couldn't tell whether he was really bragging, or just teasing you.

Children who brought home poor grades were made to study during the afternoon, and were tutored by the older ones and Mother and Dad. But Dad seldom scolded for this offense. He was convinced that the low marks were merely an error of judgment on the teacher's part.

"That teacher must not know her business," he'd grumble for Mother's benefit. "Imagine failing one of my children. Why she doesn't even have the sense to tell a smart child from a moron."

When we moved to Montclair, the business of enrolling us in the public schools was first on the agenda. Dad loaded seven of us in the Pierce Arrow and started out.

"Follow me, Live Bait," he said. "I'm going to enjoy this. We are going to descend upon the halls of learning. Remember, this is one of the most important experiences of your life. Make the most of it and keep your eyes and ears open. Let me do the talking."

The first stop was Nishuane, the elementary school, an imposing and forbidding structure of dark red brick. At its front were two doors, one marked "Boys," the other "Girls."

"Frank, Bill, Lill and Fred—this is your school," said Dad. "Come on, in we go. No dying cow looks. Hold your shoulders straight and look alive."

We piled out, hating it.

"You older girls, too," said Dad. "We may as well make an impression."

"Oh, no, Daddy."

"What's the matter with you? Come on!"

"But this isn't our school."

"I know it, but we may as well show them what a real family looks like. Wonder if I have time to run home and get your Mother and the babies."

That was enough to cause the older girls to jump quickly out of the car.

As we approached the door marked "Boys," the girls turned and started for the other entrance.

"Here, where are you girls going?" Dad asked.

"This is the girls' door over this way."

"Nonsense," said Dad. "We don't have to pay any attention to those foolish rules. What are they trying to do here, anyway? Regiment the kids?"

"Hush, Daddy. They'll hear you."

"Suppose they do. They're going to hear from me soon enough, anyway."

We all went in through the door marked "Boys." Classes already were in session, and you could see the children watching us through the open doors as we walked down the corridor to the principal's office. One teacher came gasping to the doorway.

"Good morning, Miss," said Dad, bowing with a flourish. "Just a Gilbreth invasion—or a partial invasion, I should say, since I left most of them at home with their mother. Beautiful morning, isn't it?"

"It certainly is," she smiled.

The principal of Nishuane was an elderly lady, almost as plump as Dad, and much shorter. She had the most refined voice in the Middle Atlantic States. Probably she was a very kind, gracious woman, but she was a principal, and we were scared of her. All but Dad.

"Good morning, Ma'am," he said, with another bow. "I'm Gilbreth."

"How do you do. I've heard of you."

"Only four of them enroll here," Dad said, nodding toward us. "I brought the other three along so that you could get a better

Vasiliu

idea of the crop we're raising. Red heads mostly. Some blondes.
All speckled."

"Just so. I'll take care of everything, Mr. Gilbreth. And I'm
glad you dropped in."

"Wait a minute," said Dad. "I'm not just dropping in. I want to
meet their teachers and see what grades they're going in. I'm not
in any hurry. I've arranged my schedule so that I can give you
my entire morning."

"I'll be glad to introduce you to the teachers, Mr. Gilbreth. As
to the classes they will enter, that depends on their ages."

"Hold on, hold on," Dad put in. "Depends on age, yes. Mental
age. Come here, Bill. How old are you? Eight, isn't it?"

Bill nodded.

"What grade do eight-year-olds usually belong in?"

"The third," the principal replied.

"I want him in the fifth, please."

"The fourth," said the principal. But you could tell that she was
beaten.

"Ma'am," said Dad. "Do you know the capital of Colombia?
Do you know the population of Des Moines, according to the
1910 census? I know you do, being the principal. So does Bill,
here. So does little Jackie, but I had to leave him home. It's time
for his bottle."

"The fifth," said the principal.

After we were enrolled came the surprise visits that we used to
dread, because Dad seemed to break all the school rules. He went
in doors marked "Out," he went up stairs marked "Down," and
he sometimes even wore his hat in the corridors. For any one of
these offenses, a child might be kept after school for a week; for
all three, he might be sent to reform school until his beard grew

down to his knees. But the teachers always seemed to enjoy Dad's visits and the attention he gave them, and the principals—even the Nishuane principal—always were after him to speak at the school assemblies.

"If you had half the sense, or the manners, of your father or your mother," the teachers used to say, when they'd scold one of us.

Sometimes the class would be right in the middle of saluting the flag, when in would burst Dad, with a grin stretching from ear to ear. Even the kindergarten children knew of the inflexible rule against entering a room while the flag was being saluted. No pupil would have dared to do so, even to spread an alarm of fire, monsoon or the black plague. Yet, there was Dad. The floor seemed to rock while you waited for Miss Billsop to bare her fangs and spring. But, instead, Miss Billsop would grin right back at him. Then Dad would salute the flag, too, and you'd hear his deep voice booming over that of the class: "One nation, indivisible, with liberty and justice for all."

Everybody in school knew that the Lord's Prayer followed the salute to the flag, and that after "justice for all" you were supposed to sit down and bow your head on your desk, with your eyes closed, waiting for the teacher to lead off with "Our Father, Who art in Heaven." And there was Dad.

"Good morning, Miss Billsop," he'd say. Then—and this was the worst of all—"Hello, Frank, Junior. I see you hiding behind that book. Sort of a surprise visit, eh? Hello, shavers. Excuse me for interrupting you. I'm Frank, Junior's, father. I won't take up much of your teacher's time. Then she can get back to the lessons I know you love so well."

The class would laugh, and Dad would laugh with them. He really loved kids.

"How is he getting along, Miss Billsop?" (Once he called her Milksop, by mistake, and sent her a dozen roses later that morning, as an apology.) "What's the story? Is he keeping up with his work? Does he need to study more at home? You're doing a fine job with him, and he's always quoting you around the house. Do you think he can skip the next grade? If he doesn't behave himself, just let me know."

Dad would listen to Miss Billsop for a few minutes, then drop you what might have been a wink, and burst out of the room again, to go to the classroom of another Gilbreth child.

Miss Billsop would still be smiling when she'd turn to the class.

"Now children, we will bow our heads, close our eyes, and repeat the Lord's Prayer."

You'd wait anxiously for recess, knowing that you were going to have to fight if anyone so much as hinted that your father was a fat man, or that he didn't know the school rules even as well as a kindergarten child. But, instead, a couple of the kids would come up shyly and tell you:

"Gee, your old man is the cat's, all right. He's not scared of anything."

"Yeah," you'd say.

Sometimes you'd try to tell Dad after such a visit that his popping in like that was embarrassing.

"Embarrassing?" he would ask a little hurt. "What's embarrassing about it?" Then he'd sort of pinch you on the shoulder and say, "Well, maybe it is a little embarrassing for me, too, Old Timer. But you've got to learn not to show it, and once you've learned that, it doesn't matter any more. The important thing is that dropping in like that gets results. The teachers lap it up."

They did, too.

Since Dad went to church only if one of us was being christened —in other words, about once a year—Mother had to carry the ball when it came to enrolling us in Sunday school. Dad said he believed in God, but that he couldn't stand clergymen.

"They give me the creeps," he said. "Show me a man with a loud mouth, a roving eye, a fat rear, and an empty head, and I'll show you a preacher."

Dad had crossed to Europe once on a liner carrying a delegation to a ministers' convention. It was on this trip that he had acquired most of his distaste for the reverends.

"They monopolized all the conversation at dinner," he complained—and it was obvious that this was the real sin he could never forgive. "They crawled out of every argument by citing the Lord God Jehovah as their authority. I was asked on an average of eight times a day, for eight miserable and consecutive days, to come to Jesus, whatever that is. And a stewardess told me that her behind had been pinched surreptitiously so many times between Hoboken and Liverpool that she had to eat off a mantelpiece."

Dad believed in Sunday school, though, because he thought everyone should have some knowledge of the Bible.

"The successful man knows something about everything," he said.

He used to drive Mother and us to Sunday school, and then sit outside in the car, reading *The New York Times* and ignoring the shocked glares of passing churchgoers.

"You at least might come in where it's warm," Mother told him. "You'll catch your death out here."

"No," Dad replied. "When I go to meet my Maker, I want to be able to tell Him that I did my praying on my own, halted by neither snow nor sleet nor icy stares, and without the aid of any black-frocked, collar-backwards cheerleader."

"You might at least park where they won't all see you."

"All the glares in Christendom won't force me to retreat," Dad said. "Besides, I'll bet I have half the town praying to save my soul."

Dad told Mother that the only church he'd even consider joining was the Catholic church.

"That's the only outfit that would give me some special credit for having such a large family," he said. "Besides, most priests whom I have known do not appear to be surreptitious pinchers."

"Like this," said Ernestine, pinching Anne where she sat down.

"You stop that," said Mother, shocked. And turning to Dad.

"You're really going to have to watch the stories you tell in front of the children. They don't miss a thing."

"The sooner they know what to expect from preachers, the better," said Dad. "Do you want to have them all eating off the mantelpiece?"

Although Mother always claimed that she liked church, she usually was ready to go home immediately after Sunday school.

"What's the matter, Lillie?" Dad would ask. "Stay around awhile. I'll take the children home and come back for you."

"No, I guess not this morning."

"You're not going to be able to get past St. Peter just on the strength of going to Sunday school, you know."

"Well, I'd be miserable up there anyway without you," Mother would smile. "Come on. Let's go home. I'll go to church next Sunday."

Mother did take an active part in the Sunday school work, though. She didn't teach a class, but she served on a number of committees. Once she called on a woman who had just moved to town, to ask her to serve on a fund-raising committee.

"I'd be glad to if I had the time," the woman said. "But I have three young sons and they keep me on the run. I'm sure if you have a boy of your own, you'll understand how much trouble three can be."

"Of course," said Mother. "That's quite all right. And I do understand."

"Have you any children, Mrs. Gilbreth?"

"Oh, yes."

"Any boys?"

"Yes, indeed."

"May I ask how many?"

"Certainly. I have six boys."

"Six boys!" gulped the woman. "Imagine a family of six!"

"Oh, there're more in the family than that. I have six girls, too."

"I surrender," whispered the newcomer. "When is the next meeting of the committee? I'll be there, Mrs. Gilbreth. I'll be there."

One teacher in the Sunday school, a Mrs. Bruce, had the next-to-largest family in Montclair. She had eight children, most of whom were older than we. Her husband was very successful in business, and they lived in a large house, about two miles from us. Mother and Mrs. Bruce became great friends.

About a year later, a New York woman connected with some sort of national birth control organization came to Montclair to form a local chapter. Her name was Mrs. Alice Mebane, or something like that. She inquired among her acquaintances as to who in Montclair might be sympathetic to the birth control movement. As a joke, someone referred her to Mrs. Bruce.

"I'd be delighted to cooperate," Mother's friend told Mrs. Mebane, "but you see I have several children myself."

"Oh, I had no idea," said Mrs. Mebane. "How many?"

"Several," Mrs. Bruce replied vaguely. "So I don't think I would be the one to head up any birth control movement in Montclair."

"I must say, I'm forced to agree. We should know where we're going, and practice what we preach."

"But I do know just the person for you," Mrs. Bruce continued. "And she has a big house that would be simply ideal for holding meetings."

"Just what we want," purred Mrs. Mebane. "What is her name?"

"Mrs. Frank Gilbreth. She's civic minded, and she's a career woman."

"Exactly what we want. Civic minded, career woman, and— most important of all—a large house. One other thing—I suppose it's too much to hope for—but is she by any chance an organizer? You know, one who can take things over and militantly drive ahead?"

"The description," gloated Mrs. Bruce, "fits her like a glove."

"It's almost too good to be true," said Mrs. Mebane, wringing her hands in ecstasy. "May I use your name and tell Mrs. Gilbreth you sent me?"

"By all means," said Mother's friend. "Please do. I shall be disappointed, if you don't."

"And don't think that I disapprove of your having children," laughed Mrs. Mebane. "After all, many people do, you know."

"Careless of them," remarked Mrs. Bruce.

The afternoon that Mrs. Mebane arrived at our house, all of us children were, as usual, either upstairs in our rooms or playing in the back yard. Mrs. Mebane introduced herself to Mother.

"It's about birth control," she told Mother.

"What about it?" Mother asked, blushing.

"I was told you'd be interested."

"Me?"

"I've just talked to your friend, Mrs. Bruce, and she was certainly interested."

"Isn't it a little late for her to be interested?" Mother asked.

"I see what you mean, Mrs. Gilbreth. But better late than never, don't you think?"

"But she has eight children," said Mother.

Mrs. Mebane blanched, and clutched her head.

"My God," she said. "Not really."

Mother nodded.

"How perfectly frightful. She impressed me as quite normal. Not at all like an eight-child woman."

"She's kept her youth well," Mother conceded.

"Ah, there's work to be done, all right," Mrs. Mebane said. "Think of it, living right here within eighteen miles of our national birth control headquarters in New York City, and her having eight children. Yes, there's work to be done, Mrs. Gilbreth, and that's why I'm here."

"What sort of work?"

"We'd like you to be the moving spirit behind a Montclair birth control chapter."

Mother decided at this point that the situation was too ludicrous for Dad to miss, and that he'd never forgive her if she didn't deal him in.

"I'll have to ask my husband," she said. "Excuse me while I call him."

Mother stepped out and found Dad. She gave him a brief

explanation and then led him into the parlor and introduced him.

"It's a pleasure to meet a woman in such a noble cause," said Dad.

"Thank you. And it's a pleasure to find a man who thinks of it as noble. In general, I find the husbands much less sympathetic with our aims than the wives. You'd be surprised at some of the terrible things men have said to me."

"I love surprises," Dad leered. "What do you say back to them?"

"If you had seen, as I have," said Mrs. Mebane, "relatively young women grown old before their time by the arrival of unwanted young ones. And population figures show . . . Why Mr. Gilbreth, what are you doing?"

What Dad was doing was whistling assembly. On the first note, feet could be heard pounding on the floors above. Doors slammed, there was a landslide on the stairs, and we started skidding into the parlor.

"Nine seconds," said Dad pocketing his stopwatch. "Three short of the all-time record."

"God's teeth," said Mrs. Mebane. "What is it? Tell me quickly. It is a school? No. Or is it . . . ? For Lord's sakes. It is!"

"It is what?" asked Dad.

"It's your family. Don't try to deny it. They're the spit and image of you, and your wife, too."

"I was about to introduce you," said Dad. "Mrs. Mebane, let me introduce you to the family—or most of it. Seems to me like there should be some more of them around here someplace."

"God help us all."

"How many head of children do we have now, Lillie, would you say off hand?"

"Last time I counted, seems to me there was an even dozen

of them," said Mother. "I might have missed one or two of them, but not many."

"I'd say twelve would be a pretty fair guess," Dad said.

"Shame on you! And within eighteen miles of national headquarters."

"Let's have tea," said Mother.

But Mrs. Mebane was putting on her coat. "You poor dear," she clucked to Mother. "You poor child." Then turning to Dad. "It seems to me that the people of this town have pulled my leg on two different occasions today."

"How revolting," said Dad. "And within eighteen miles of national headquarters, too."

CHAPTER 8

Kissing Kin

THE day the United States entered the first World War, Dad sent President Wilson a telegram which read: "Arriving Washington 7:03 p.m. train. If you don't know how to use me, I'll tell you how."

Whether or not this heartening intelligence took some of the weight off Mr. Wilson's troubled shoulders, Dad never made entirely plain. But he was met at the train and taken over to the War Department. The next time we saw him, he was in uniform, assigned to motion study training in assembling and disassembling the Lewis machine gun and other automatic weapons. He had what probably was the most G.I. haircut in the entire armed forces, and when he walked into the parlor and shouted "Attention!" he wanted to hear our heels click.

Mother had been planning for several years to take all of us to

California to visit her family. When Dad was ordered to Fort Sill, Oklahoma, the time seemed opportune.

Mother's family was genteel and well-to-do. She was the oldest of nine children, only three of whom were married. The other six, two brothers and four sisters, lived with their parents in a spacious house at 426 Twenty-Ninth Street, in Oakland. The house was fringed with palm trees, magnificent gardens, and concealed but nonetheless imposing outbuildings in which the family indulged its various hobbies. There were a billiard hall, radio shack, greenhouse, pigeon roost, and a place where prize-winning guinea pigs were raised.

The Mollers had three Packards, a French chauffeur named Henriette, a gardener, Chinese cook, first-story maid, and second-story maid. The Mollers managed, somehow, in spite of their worldly goods, to live fairly simply. They were quiet, introverted, and conservative. They seldom raised their voices and referred to each other as "Dear Elinor, Dear Mabel, Dear Gertrude," and so on. Mother was "Dear Lillie."

Mother was the only one in her family who had moved from California. Mother had left home after her marriage, as introverted and conservative, and possibly even more shy and bookish, than any of the others. In ten years, she had seven children. She was lecturing around the country. She was a career woman and her name kept bobbing up in the newspapers. Frankly, the Mollers didn't know exactly what to make of Dear Lillie. But they knew they loved her.

Even before we visited California, we knew all about the household at Oakland and its inhabitants, because Mother used to like to tell us about her girlhood. We knew the arrangement of the house, even down to the full-length mirror on the hall door, which

Mother's younger sisters used to open at just the right angle so that they could watch Dad's courting technique.

Hearing Mother tell about the courtship, the sparking on the sofa, we used to wonder what Mother's parents had thought when Dad first came to call.

He had met Mother in Boston, about a year before, when she was on that well-chaperoned tour to Europe, with several other Oakland girls. The chaperone, who was Dad's cousin, had introduced him to all the girls, but he had selected Miss Lillie as the one on whom to shower his attention.

He took Mother for a ride in his first automobile, some early ancestor of Foolish Carriage. As Dad and Mother, dressed in dusters and wearing goggles, went scorching through the streets of Boston, bystanders tossed insults and ridicule in their direction.

"Get a horse, get a horse."

Dad started to shout back an answer, but thought better of it. He was already in love with Mother, and was anxious to make a good impression. Mother's shyness and ladylike demeanor had a quieting effect on him, and he was displaying his most genteel behavior.

"Get a horse. Twenty-three skiddoo."

It was almost more than Dad could bear, but he didn't answer.

"Say, Noah, what are you doing with that Ark?"

That did it. Dad slowed the car and cocked his checkered cap belligerently over one eye.

"Collecting animals like the good Lord told me," he screamed back. "All I need now is a jackass. Hop in."

After that, Dad decided he might as well be himself, and his breezy personality and quick laugh made Mother forget her shyness and reserve. Soon she found herself laughing almost as loud and as long at his jokes as he.

As was its custom, the automobile inevitably broke down, and crowds of children gathered around. Mother stopped them from breathing down Dad's neck by taking them aside and telling them stories. When the car was fixed and they were on their way again, Dad asked her how she had managed to hold the children's attention.

"I told them some stories from *Alice in Wonderland*," Mother said. "You see, I have eight younger brothers and sisters, and I know what children like."

"*Alice in Wonderland*," Dad exclaimed. "You mean kids really like that? They must be raising different kinds of kids than when I was a boy. I never could get into it, myself."

"Of course they like it; they love it," Mother said. "You really should read it. I think everybody should. It's a classic."

"If you say so, Miss Lillie," said Dad, who had already made up his mind she was going to be Mrs. Gilbreth, "I'll read it."

Mother went on to Europe. After her return, Dad followed her out to the West Coast.

When he arrived at Oakland, he telephoned the Mollers' house.

"Hello," he said, "who do you think this is?"

"Really, I have no idea."

"Well guess, can't you?"

"No, I'm sorry, I have no idea."

"Aw, you know who it is," said Dad, who now had read the book that Mother said everyone should read. "It's the White Rabbit from Boston."

"The who?"

"The White Rabbit from Boston."

"Oh, I see. I think you must want to talk with one of my daughters."

"My God," said Dad, who didn't stop swearing until after he was married. "Who's this?"

"This is Mrs. Moller. To whom did you wish to speak?"

"May I please speak with Miss Lillie?" Dad asked meekly.

"Who should I say is calling?"

"You might say Mr. Rabbit, please," said Dad. "Mr. W. Rabbit, of Boston."

A few days later, Dad was invited to Mother's house for tea, where he met her mother and father and most of her brothers and sisters. A workman was building a new fireplace in the living room, and as Dad was escorted through that room he stopped to watch the man laying bricks.

"Now there's an interesting job," Dad said in a conversational tone to the Mollers. "Laying brick. It looks easy to me. Dead easy. I don't see why these workmen claim that laying brick is skilled labor. I'll bet anyone could do it."

"Right this way, Mr. Gilbreth," said Mother's father. "We're having tea on the porch."

Dad wouldn't be hurried. "It seems to me," he continued in his flat New England twang, "that all you do is pick up a brick, put some mortar on it, and put it in the fireplace."

The bricklayer turned around to survey the plump but dapper dude from the East.

"Nothing personal meant," said Dad, with his most patronizing smile, "my good man."

"Sure, that's all right," said the workman, but he was furious. "Dead easy, eh? Like to try it, Mister?"

Dad, who had set his sights on just such an invitation, said he guessed not. Mother tugged at his sleeve and fidgeted.

"The porch is right this way," her father repeated.

"Here," the bricklayer said, handing Dad the trowel. "Try it."

Dad grinned and took the trowel. He grabbed a brick, flipped it into position in his hand, slapped on the mortar with a rotary motion of the trowel, placed the brick, scraped off the excess mortar, reached for a second brick, flipped it, and was about to slap on more mortar when the workman reached out and took back his trowel.

"That's enough, you old hod-carrier," he shouted, cuffing Dad affectionately on the back. "Dude from the East you might be. But it's many a thousand brick you've laid in your life, and don't try to tell me different."

Dad dusted off his hands gingerly with a spotless handkerchief.

"Dead easy," he said, "my good man."

Dad behaved himself pretty well during the tea, but on later visits he'd sometimes interrupt Mother's parents in the middle of sentences and go over and pick up Mother from her chair.

"Excuse me just a minute," he'd tell his future in-laws. "I think Miss Lillie would look more decorative up here."

He'd swing her up and place her on the top of a bookcase or china closet, and then go back and sit down. Mother was afraid to move for fear of upsetting her perch, and would remain up there primly, determined not to lose her dignity. Dad pretended he had forgotten all about her, as he resumed the conversation.

We knew, too, that the first time Dad had been invited to spend a weekend at the Mollers he had thrown himself with a wheeze and a sigh onto his bed, which had collapsed and enveloped him in a heavy, be-tasseled canopy.

"The things your daddy shouted before Papa and your Uncle Fred could untangle him from the tassels!" Mother tittered. "I can tell you, it was an education for us girls and, I suspect, for the boys too. Thank goodness he's stopped talking like that."

"And what did your family really think of him?" we asked her. "Really."

"I never could understand it," Mother said, glancing over at Dad, who was at his smuggest, "but they thought he was simply wonderful. Mama said it was like a breath of fresh air when he walked into a room. And Papa said the business of laying bricks wasn't just showing off, but was your father's way of telling them that he had started out by making a living with his hands."

"Is that what you were trying to tell them, Daddy?" we asked.

"Trying to tell them nothing," Dad shouted. "Anybody who knows anything about New England knows the Bunkers and the Gilbreths, or Galbraiths, descend through Governor Bradford right to the *Mayflower*. I wasn't trying to tell them anything."

"What did you lay the brick for then?" we insisted.

"When some people walk into a parlor," Dad said, "they like to sit down at the piano and impress people by playing Bach. When I walk into a parlor, I like to lay brick, that's all."

There were seven children in the family when we set out with Mother for California. Fred was the baby, and was train sick all the way from Niagara Falls to the Golden Gate. Lill, the next to youngest, had broken a bone in her foot three weeks before, and had to stay in her berth. Mother was expecting another baby in three months, and didn't always feel too well herself.

The chance to return with her children to her parents' home meant more to Mother than any of us realized. and she was anxious

Vasiliu

to show us off in the best possible light and to have her family approve of us.

"I know you're going to be good and quiet, and do what your grandparents and your aunts and uncles tell you," Mother kept saying. "You want to remember that they're very affectionate, but they're not accustomed to having children around any more. They're going to love you, but they're not used to noise and people running around."

Mother had spent a good bit of money buying us new outfits so that we would make a good impression in California, and she thought she ought to economize on train accommodations. We were jammed, two in a berth, into a drawing room and two sections. She brought along a Sterno cooking outfit and two suitcases of food, mostly cereals and graham crackers. We ate almost all our meals in the drawing room, journeying to the dining car only on those infrequent occasions when Mother yielded to our complaints that scurvy was threatening to set in.

She spent most of her time trying to make Lill comfortable and trying to find some kind of milk that would stay on Fred's stomach. She had little opportunity to supervise the rest of us, and we wandered up and down the train sampling the contents of the various ice water tanks, peeking into berths and, in the case of Frank and Bill, turning somersaults and wrestling with each other in the aisles.

At each stop, Mother would leave Anne in charge of the broken foot and upset stomach department, while she rushed into the station to buy milk, food, and Sterno cans. The rest of us would get off the train to stretch our legs and see whether a new engine had been switched on. Once the train started up again, Mother would insist upon a roll call.

After four days on the train, with no baths except for the sponge variety, we were not very sanitary when we reached California. Mother wanted us to look our best when we got off the train, and she planned to give each of us a personal scrubbing and see that we had on clean clothes, an hour or so before we got to Oakland.

Her oldest brother, Uncle Fred, surprised her and us by boarding the train at Sacramento. He found us in the drawing room, in the middle of a meal. Suitcases were open on the floor, and there was a pile of diapers in a corner. The baby, still train sick, was crying in Mother's arms. Lill's foot was hurting, and she was crying on the couch. Bill was doing acrobatics on the bed. There were bowls of Cream of Wheat and graham crackers on a card table. The place smelled of Sterno and worse.

Uncle Fred used to joke about it when we were older—it reminded him of a zoo, he said. But at the time you never would have known he noticed anything unusual.

"Lillie, dear, it's good to see you," he said. "You look simply radiant. Not a day older."

"Oh, Fred, Fred." Mother put down the baby, wiped her eyes apologetically, and clung to her brother. "It's ridiculous to cry, isn't it? But it means so much having you here."

"Was it a hard trip, dear?"

Mother was already bustling around, straightening up the drawing room.

"I wouldn't want to do it every day," she admitted. "But it's almost over and you're here. You're my first taste of home."

Uncle Fred turned to us. "Welcome to California," he said "Don't tell me now. I can name each of you. Let's see, the baby here making all the noise, he's my namesake, Fred. And here's little Lill, of course, with the broken foot, and Billy . . ."

"You're just like we imagined you," Martha told him, hanging onto his hand. "Are we like you imagined us?"

"Just exactly," he said gravely. "Right down to the last freckle."

"I hope you didn't imagine them like this," Mother said, but she was happy now. "Never mind. You'll never know them in a few minutes. You take the boys out into the car, and I'll start getting the girls cleaned up right now. Of course, none of them will be really clean until I can get them into a tub."

We were presentable and on our best behavior when we finally arrived in Oakland, where Mother's sisters and other brothers were waiting with the three limousines. It was a wonderful welcome, but we thought our aunts were the kissingest kin in the world.

"They must think we're sissies," whispered Bill, who was five and didn't like to be kissed by anyone except Mother, and only then in the privacy of his boudoir.

"Lillie, dear, it's good to see you, and the dear children," they kept repeating.

Each of us had a godparent among Mother's brothers and sisters, and now the godparents began sorting us out.

"Here, little Ernestine, you come with me, dear," said Aunt Ernestine.

"Come, Martha, dear," said Aunt Gertrude. "You're mine."

"Give me your hand, Frank, dear," said Aunt Elinor.

"Dear this and dear that," Billy whispered scornfully.

"Where's dear Billy?" asked Aunt Mabel.

"Right here, dear," said Bill.

But Bill, like the rest of us, felt happy and warm inside because of the welcome.

The aunts led us over to the automobiles, where Henriette, in black puttees and with a stiff-brimmed cap tucked under his arm, was standing at rigid attention. Uncle Frank and Uncle Bill got behind the wheels of the other two machines.

The glassed-in cars seemed formal and luxurious as we drove from the station to Twenty-Ninth Street, and Henriette managed to remain at attention even when sitting down. We wondered what Daddy would say about Henriette. Certainly rigid attention wasn't the most efficient way to drive an automobile. Anyone with half an eye could see the posture was fatiguing to the point of exhaustion. It was some class, though.

Frank and Bill started to crank down the windows so they could put out their hands when he turned the corners, but Anne and Ernestine shook their heads.

"And the first one who hollers 'road hog' is going to get a punch in the nose," Ernestine whispered.

Mother's father and mother—Papa and Grosie, we called them—were waiting for us on the steps of the house. We thought they were picture-book grandparents. Papa was tall, lean and courtly, with a gates-ajar collar, string tie, and soft, white moustache. Grosie was short and fragile, with a gray pompadour and smiling brown eyes. Grosie kissed us and called us "dears." Papa shook hands, and said that each day we stayed in his house he was going to take all of us down to a toy shop and let us pick out a toy apiece.

"Honestly," Anne bubbled, "it's like stepping into a fairy tale three-deep with godmothers and with wishes that come true."

"That's the way we want it to be for Lillie's dear children," Grosie said. "Now what's your very first wish. Tell me, and I'll see if I can make it come true."

That was easy. After four days of Mother's drawing room cookery, with only infrequent trips to the dining car, what we wanted most was something good to eat; a real home-cooked meal.

"I hate to say it after the way Mother's been slaving over a hot Sterno can," said Ernestine, "but we're starving."

"If my wish would come true," Mother hastened to change the subject, "you'd all be sitting in bathtubs right this minute, washing soot out of your hair."

Grosie said we were going to have a big dinner in about an hour and a half, and that she didn't want to spoil our appetites.

"How about just a little snack right now," she suggested, "and then baths and dinner? How about some graham crackers with milk? I know how much little children like graham crackers, and we have a great big supply of them."

The mention of graham crackers took away our appetites, and we said we guessed we'd skip the snack and get our baths.

"Such dear children," Grosie squeezed us. "They want their dear Mother's wish to come true!"

CHAPTER 9

Chinese Cooking

WE were so impressed by the comforts and quiet organization of the Mollers' home that we were subdued and on our best behavior. But the biggest change was in Mother. Ensconced again in the bedroom in which she had grown up, she seemed to shed her responsibilities and become again "one of the Moller girls." Automatically, she found herself depending on her father to make the important decisions, and on her mother to advise her on social engagements and the proper clothes to wear. She seemed to have forgotten all about motion study, her career, and the household back East. Her principal worries seemed to be whether her parents had slept well, how they were feeling, whether they were sitting in drafts.

"Mama, dear," she'd say, "are you sure that shawl is warm enough? Let me run upstairs and get you another."

Since Mother seemed so concerned about Grosie and Papa, we held them in awe. We tiptoed in their presence and talked only in whispers.

The respect in which we held Grosie was heightened the day after our arrival, when she gave Mother a quiet reprimand which Mother accepted just as if she were a little girl again. Anybody who could have that effect on Mother, we thought, must be a very important person.

The reprimand came about after Grosie handed Mother a list of six close friends of the family, and suggested that Mother call to pay her respects that afternoon.

"Do you really think it's necessary, Mama, dear?" Mother asked.

"I think it would be nice, dear."

"What do you think I should wear?"

"I would think the dress you wore to dinner last night would be just right, dear."

Mother set out to make the calls, and returned about two hours later.

"There," she said, coming smiling into the living room. "Thank goodness that's out of the way. It didn't take me long, did it? Six calls in two hours! Wasn't I efficient?"

To be efficient, in the Gilbreth family, was a virtue on a par with veracity, honesty, generosity, philanthropy, and tooth-brushing. We agreed that Mother had, indeed, been exceptionally efficient. But Grosie looked disapproving.

"Don't you think I was efficient, Mama, dear?"

"Perhaps, Lillie, dear," Grosie said slowly, "perhaps you were a little—too—efficient."

Our grandparents became worried by our exemplary behavior. They told Mother they didn't think it was natural, and that it made them nervous the way we tiptoed and whispered.

"They don't act at all the way I pictured them," Papa said. "From your letters, I thought they whooped and hollered around. I don't believe they feel at home."

"They'll feel at home soon enough," Mother warned. "I'm scared that when they decide to feel at home they may decide all at once. If they do, it's Katey bar the door."

We decided to feel at home on the day that Grosie gave a formal tea in Mother's honor. Our godmothers had bathed us with sweet-smelling soap and were dressing us in new outfits that Grosie had approved. For the girls, it was dotted Swiss and matching hair ribbons and sashes; for the boys, blue serge suits and Buster Brown collars, with red, generous bow ties.

The boys' trousers were shorts, rather than knickers, and buttoned down the sides, instead of down the front. That was bad enough, Frank and Bill thought. But the crowning indignity was a little flap, like the tongue of a shoe sewed on sideways, that served as a fly at the front of the trousers.

"We're all going to be so proud of you today, dears," the aunts told us. "I know you're going to make such a lovely impression on all the guests."

"Not in these pants," Bill said. "I look sissy and I'm not going to wear them."

"Why Billy, dear," said Aunt Mabel, his godmother. "You look lovely. You look just like Little Lord Fauntleroy."

"I don't want to look like him," Bill shouted. "I'm not going to wear these clothes."

"Of course you're going to wear them, Billy, dear. What do you think your father would say to hear you talk like that?"

"I think he'd say they were sissy, too," said Bill. "I think he'd laugh at the flap on the front of my pants."

"Be a good boy, now, dear. You don't want to worry your mother and Grosie and Papa."

"I do too," said Bill. "I'm sick of not worrying people. I say to heck with them."

The godmothers froze.

"Why Billy Gilbreth," said Aunt Mabel. "Where did you learn such an *ugly* word?"

We thought for just a moment that we saw a trace of a grin pass over Aunt Mabel's face, and that Aunt Gertrude nudged Aunt Ernestine, but we dismissed the notion as highly improbable and extremely out-of-character.

Bill finally was prevailed upon to dress in his new outfit. But he was sullen, and so were the rest of us when we received our instructions about the party.

"First the grownups will have a little chat and visit by themselves, dears. Then we want you children to come in and meet the guests. Remember, some of these people are your mother's oldest friends, and she wants to be proud of you, so do be careful about your clothes. Now run along out into the garden, and we'll call you when it's time."

Left by ourselves, we walked out on the lawn, where we formed a starched, uncomfortable, and resentful group. We were tired of being on our best behavior, and we wished Daddy were there to stir up some excitement.

"At home," Martha whispered to the rest of us, "the children visit when the grownups visit. They don't have to go stand in the garden like darned lepers."

"Why, Martha, dear," Ern mimicked, in shocked tones, "Where did you learn such an *ugly* word?"

"At home," said Martha, "they think the children have enough sense to fix their own hair. And they don't have to wear hair ribbons tied so tight that they can't wiggle their eyebrows."

"Look at the flap in the front of the pants," said Bill, pointing.

A sprinkler was watering the lawn nearby. Martha jerked off her hair ribbon, threw it on the ground, walked deliberately to the sprinkler and stood under it.

Anne and Ernestine were horrified. "Martha," they shouted. "Are you crazy? Come out of there."

Martha put her head back and laughed. She opened her mouth and caught water in it. She wiggled her now free eyebrows in ecstasy. The starch went out of her clothes, and her hair streamed over her face.

Frank and Bill joined Martha under the sprinkler. Then Ernestine came in, thus leaving Anne, the oldest, in what for her was a fairly familiar dilemma: Whether to cast her lot with us or with the adults. She knew that being the oldest she'd be held responsible, whichever course she took.

"Come in and get wet," we shouted. "Don't be a traitor. The water's fine."

Anne sighed, untied her hair ribbon and came in.

"All right, dears," one of the aunts called from the house. "It's time to meet the guests now."

We filed, into the living room, where our dripping clothes made puddles on Grosie's Persian rug.

"I think they feel at home now," Mother said a little ruefully. "You children listen to me. Go upstairs and change your clothes. No nonsense, now. I want you down here, dry, in ten minutes. Do you understand?"

We understood. That was the kind of talk we understood.

Everybody liked it better now that we went shouting through the house, playing hide-and-go-seek, and sliding down the banisters. Only during the afternoons, when Grosie was taking a nap, Papa asked us to be quiet.

"Try to keep it down to a dull roar for just two hours, dears," he told us. "Your grandmother really needs her rest."

Our godmothers waited on us hand and foot, and we began to enjoy and even revel in the attention. They were willing to drop anything to amuse us, to play games with us, to help us plant a flower garden, to paste in our scrap books, to collect California seeds which we intended to plant in our yard when we returned home. They took us to the movies, on sightseeing tours to Chinatown in San Francisco, and away for weekends at their summer cottage at Inverness. It seemed natural now for them to call us "dears," and we began to return the salutation without sarcasm or affectation. When dear Aunt Gertrude had herself hospitalized because she was afraid she was coming down with whooping cough and didn't want to infect us, we mourned her departure almost as if she had been Mother herself.

Bill, meanwhile, had found a devoted friend and ally in the kitchen, where Chew Wong's word was law. Chew Wong was set in his ways and unamenable to suggestion. He was sinister looking and uncommunicative, and had a terrible temper. He understood English fairly well, except when someone tried to criticize him or tell him what to do. In such cases he launched into hissing Chinese, brandished skillets, and then turned his back and walked away. He was a wonderful cook. It was tacitly understood in the Moller family that the less one knew about his cooking methods and what he put into the food, the better for all concerned.

Of the Mollers, only Aunt Elinor, who planned the menus, ventured into the kitchen. We children were advised to keep out of it unless we wished to invoke Oriental wrath, die in agony from some exotic poison, touch off a tong war, or go through life with the responsibility of hara-kiri hanging over our heads.

Although aware of the possible consequences, Bill couldn't resist the smell of cakes and pies, and began to spend a good deal of his time in the kitchen. At first Aunt Elinor would hustle him out. But Chew Wong had taken a liking to him, and sulked when Bill was removed. Whenever Chew Wong sulked, his cooking suffered, and it finally was decided to allow Bill the run of the kitchen.

Chew Wong outdid himself then with the meals that he served up, and the kitchen rang with pidgin English and cackling laughter.

"Pleez now, Bleely, open mouth. Hi-hi-hi-hi-hi. Good boy, Bleely."

We questioned Bill about what he opened his mouth for. He told us that when Chew Wong iced a cake he put the frosting in a cornucopia made of newspaper, bit off the end and squeezed the frosting onto the cake. At intervals, Bill would open his mouth and the cornucopia would be inserted. When the rest of us dropped into the kitchen to get a turn at the business end of the cornucopia, Chew Wong drove us out with a skillet, while he and Bill screamed with laughter. Hi-hi-hi-hi-hi.

Sometimes, when Bill got into mischief in the kitchen, Chew

Wong scolded him, picked him up, and threatened to put him in the oven. The cook opened the oven door and put Bill part way in it, where he could feel the heat on his face.

"Blad boy, Bleely. Putee in oven and cookee brown and eatee. Hi-hi-hi."

Bill knew it was a game, but it used to scare him, and he struggled and kicked.

One afternoon Chew Wong opened the oven door and was leaning in, on tiptoe, to see whether a cake was browning on all sides. Bill crept up behind him, placed a shoulder against his rear and hunched. Then he held him there.

"Blad boy, Wong," he said in a sing-song imitation of the cook. "Bleely putee in oven and cookee brown and eatee. Hi-hi-hi-hi."

Aunt Elinor was in the pantry and heard the conversation and Chew Wong's screams. By the time she rushed into the kitchen, the cook had extricated himself, had both hands under the cold water faucet, and was squealing with rage. Other Mollers and Gilbreths converged on the kitchen from various parts of the house.

Since she was responsible for the kitchen, Aunt Elinor decided it was up to her to take Bill to task.

"Billy Gilbreth," she said almost sternly. "You haven't behaved like a gentleman."

The visit came to an end, and we put on our traveling clothes and climbed again into the limousines. We were accustomed to them now, and we didn't hesitate to roll down the windows, put out our hands, and tell road hogs what we thought of them. The Mollers didn't seem to mind; they seemed to enjoy it. Even Henriette, still at rigid attention, grinned when hands popped out as he wheeled his car sedately around the corners.

We said goodbye on the station platform. It didn't seem sissy to Bill to be kissed now. He returned the kisses.

We got on the train and pressed our noses against the glass.

"One thing I can't get over," Anne said. "They really hate to see us go. Imagine! They're crying just as hard as we are."

The train pulled out of the station, and Mother did her best to cheer us up.

"I didn't bring a single Sterno can with me," she said. "Things will be much better going home than they were coming out. Lill's foot is all better, and I don't think Freddy's going to be sick any more. We can go into the diner and . . ."

"Whoop," Martha coughed. "Whoop. Whoop."

"You don't suppose that child's caught whooping cough, do you?" Mother asked. "Let me feel your forehead."

By the time we reached Salt Lake City, all seven of us had whooping cough. Our berths couldn't be made up, and no one in the same car with us got much sleep.

Dad had managed to obtain leave from Fort Sill, and surprised us by boarding the train at Chicago. He helped with a bucket and mop Mother had borrowed from the porter, and brought us soup heated over recently acquired Sterno cans.

"Thank you, Daddy, dear," we told him.

"Daddy, dear?" he said. "Daddy, dear? Well! I guess I ought to send you kids to California every summer."

"Not with me, you don't," Mother put in. "I can't tell you how much I enjoyed seeing the dear folks. But the next time you take the children out West, and I'll go to war."

CHAPTER 10

Motion Study Tonsils

DAD thought the best way to deal with sickness in the family was simply to ignore it.

"We don't have time for such nonsense," he said. "There are too many of us. A sick person drags down the performance of the entire group. You children come from sound pioneer stock. You've been given health, and it's your job to keep it. I don't want any excuses. I want you to stay well."

Except for measles and whooping cough, we obeyed orders. Doctors' visits were so infrequent we learned to identify them with Mother's having a baby.

Dad's mother, who lived with us for awhile, had her own secret for warding off disease. Grandma Gilbreth was born in Maine, where she said the seasons were Winter, July and August.

She claimed to be an expert in combatting cold weather and in avoiding head colds.

Her secret prophylaxis was a white bag, filled and saturated with camphor, which she kept hidden in her bosom. Grandma's bosom offered ample hiding space not only for the camphor but for her eyeglasses, her handkerchief, and, if need be, for the bedspread she was crocheting.

Each year, as soon as the first frost appeared, she made twelve identical white, camphor-filled bags for each of us.

"Mind what Grandma says and wear these all the time," she told us. "Now if you bring home a cold it will be your own blessed fault, and I'll skin you alive."

Grandma always was threatening to skin someone alive, or draw and quarter him, or scalp him like a red Indian, or spank him till his bottom blistered.

Grandma averred she was a great believer in "spare the rod and spoil the child." Her own personal rod was a branch from a lilac bush, which grew in the side lawn. She always kept a twig from this bush on the top of her dresser.

"I declare, you're going to catch it now," she would say. "Your mother won't spank you and your father is too busy to spank you, but your grandma is going to spank you till your bottom blisters."

Then she would swing the twig with a vigor which belied her years. Most of her swings were aimed so as merely to whistle harmlessly through the air. She'd land a few light licks on our legs, though, and since we didn't want to hurt her feelings we'd scream and holler as if we were receiving the twenty-one lashes from a Spanish inquisitor. Sometimes she'd switch so vigorously at nothing that the twig would break.

"Ah, you see? You were so bad that I had to break my whip on you. Now go right out in the yard and cut me another one for next time. A big, thick one that will hurt even more than this one. Go along now. March!"

On the infrequent occasions when one of us did become sick enough to stay in bed, Grandma and Dad thought the best treatment was the absent treatment.

"A child abed mends best if left to himself," Grandma said, while Dad nodded approval. Mother said she agreed, too, but then she proceeded to wait on the sick child hand and foot.

"Here, darling, put my lovely bed jacket around your shoulders," Mother would tell the ailing one. "Here are some magazines, and scissors and paste. Now how's that? I'm going down to the kitchen and fix you a tray. Then I'll be up and read to you."

A cousin brought measles into the house, and all of us except Martha were stricken simultaneously. Two big adjoining bedrooms upstairs were converted into hospital wards—one for the boys and the other for the girls. We suffered together for two or three miserable, feverish, itchy days, while Mother applied cocoa butter and ice packs. Dr. Burton, who had delivered most of us, said there was nothing to worry about. He was an outspoken man, and he and Dad understood each other.

"I'll admit, Gilbreth, that your children don't get sick very often," Dr. Burton said, "but when they do it messes up the public health statistics for the entire state of New Jersey."

"How come, Mr. Bones?" Dad asked.

"I have to turn in a report every week on the number of contagious diseases I handle. Ordinarily, I handle a couple of cases of measles a week. When I report that I had eleven cases in a single day, they're liable to quarantine the whole town of Montclair and close up every school in Essex County."

"Well, they're probably exceptionally light cases." Dad said. "Pioneer stock, you know."

"As far as I'm concerned, measles is measles, and they've got the measles."

"Probably even pioneers got the measles," Dad said.

"Probably so. Pioneers had tonsils, too, and so do your kids. Really ugly tonsils. They ought to come out."

"I never had mine out."

"Let me see them," Dr. Burton ordered.

"There's nothing the matter with them."

"For God's sake don't waste my time," said Dr. Burton. "Open your mouth and say 'Ah'."

Dad opened his mouth and said "Ah."

"I thought so," Dr. Burton nodded. "Yours ought to come out too. Should have had them taken out years ago. I don't expect you to admit it, but you have sore throats, don't you? You have one right this minute, haven't you?"

"Nonsense," said Dad. "Never sick a day in my life."

"Well, let yours stay in if you want. You're not hurting anybody but yourself. But you really should have the children's taken out."

"I'll talk it over with Lillie," Dad promised.

Once the fever from the measles had gone, we all felt fine, although we still had to stay in bed. We sang songs, told continued stories, played spelling games and riddles, and had pillow fights. Dad spent considerable time with us, joining in the songs and all the games except pillow fights, which were illegal. He still

believed in letting sick children alone, but with all of us sick—
or all but Martha, at any rate—he became so lonesome he couldn't
stay away.

He came into the wards one night after supper, and took a
chair over in a corner. We noticed that his face was covered with
spots.

"Daddy," asked Anne, "what's the matter with you? You're all
broken out in spots."

"You're imagining things," said Dad, smirking. "I'm all right."

"You've got the measles."

"I'm all right," said Dad. "I can take it."

"Daddy's got the measles, Daddy's got the measles." Dad sat
there grinning, but our shouts were enough to bring Grandma
on the run.

"What's the matter here?" she asked. And then to Dad. "Mercy
sakes, Frank, you're covered with spots."

"It's just a joke," Dad told his mother, weakly.

"Get yourself to bed. A man your age ought to know better.
Shame on you."

Grandma fumbled down her dress and put on her glasses. She
peered into Dad's face.

"I declare, Frank Gilbreth," she told him, "sometimes I think
you're more trouble than all of your children. Red ink! And you
think it's a joke to scare a body half to death. Red ink!"

"A joke," Dad repeated.

"Very funny," Grandma muttered as she stalked out of the
room. "I'm splitting my sides."

Dad sat there glumly.

"Is it red ink, Daddy?" we asked, and we agreed with him that
it was, indeed, a very good joke. "Is it? You really had us fooled."

"You'll have to ask your grandma," Dad sulked. "She's a very smart lady. She knows it all."

Martha, who appeared immune to measles, nevertheless wasn't allowed to come into the wards. She couldn't go to school, since the house was quarantined, and the week or two of being an "only child" made her so miserable that she lost her appetite. Finally, she couldn't stand it any more, and sneaked into the sick rooms to visit us.

"You know you're not allowed in here," said Anne. "Do you want to get sick?"

Martha burst into tears. "Yes," she sobbed. "Oh, yes."

"Don't tell us you miss us? Why I should think it would be wonderful to have the whole downstairs to yourself, and to be able to have Mother and Dad all by yourself at dinner."

"Dad's no fun any more," said Mart. "He's nervous. He says the quiet at the table is driving him crazy."

"Tell him that's not of general interest," said Ern.

It was shortly after the measles epidemic that Dad started applying motion study to surgery to try to reduce the time required for certain operations.

"Surgeons really aren't much different from skilled mechanics," Dad said, "except that they're not so skilled. If I can get to study their motions, I can speed them up. The speed of an operation often means the difference between life and death."

At first, the surgeons he approached weren't very cooperative.

"I don't think it will work," one doctor told him. "We aren't dealing with machines. We're dealing with human beings. No two human beings are alike, so no set of motions could be used over and over again."

"I know it will work," Dad insisted. "Just let me take some moving pictures of operations and I'll show you."

Finally he got permission to set up his movie equipment in an operating room. After the film was developed he put it in the projector which he kept in the parlor and showed us what he had done.

In the background was a cross-section screen and a big clock with "GILBRETH" written across its face and a hand which made a full revolution every second. Each doctor and nurse was dressed in white, and had a number on his cap to identify him. The patient was on an operating table in the foreground. Off to the left, clad in a white sheet, was something that resembled a snow-covered Alp. When the Alp turned around, it had a stop-watch in its hand. And when it smiled at the camera you could tell through the disguise that it was Dad.

It seemed to us, watching the moving pictures, that the doctors did a rapid, business-like job of a complicated abdominal operation. But Dad, cranking the projector in back of us, kept hollering that it was "stupidity incorporated."

"Look at that boob—the doctor with No. 3 on his cap. Watch what he's going to do now. Walk all the way around the operating table. Now see him reach way over there for that instrument? And then he decides that he doesn't want that one after all. He wants this one. He should call the instrument's name, and that nurse— No. 6, she's his caddy—should hand it to him. That's what she's there for. And look at his left hand—dangling there at his side. Why doesn't he use it? He could work twice as fast."

The result of the moving picture was that the surgeons involved managed to reduce their ether time by fifteen per cent. Dad was far from satisfied. He explained that he needed to take moving pictures of five or six operations, all of the same type, so that he could sort out the good motions from the wasted motions. The trouble was that most patients refused to be photographed, and hospitals were afraid of law suits.

"Never mind, dear," Mother told him. "I'm sure the opportunity will come along eventually for you to get all the pictures that you want."

Dad said that he didn't like to wait; that when he started a project, he hated to put it aside and pick it up again piecemeal whenever he found a patient, hospital, and doctor who didn't object to photographs. Then an idea hit him, and he snapped his fingers.

"I know," he said. "I've got it. Dr. Burton has been after me to have the kids' tonsils out. He says they really have to come out. We'll rig up an operating room in the laboratory here, and take pictures of Burton."

"It seems sort of heartless to use the children as guinea pigs," Mother said doubtfully.

"It does for a fact. And I won't do it unless Burton says it's perfectly all right. If taking pictures is going to make him nervous or anything, we'll have the tonsils taken out without the motion study."

"Somehow or other I can't imagine Dr. Burton being nervous," Mother said.

"Me either. I'm going to call him. And you know what? I feel a little guilty about this whole deal. So, as conscience balm, I'm going to let the old butcher take mine out, too."

"I feel a little guilty about the whole deal, too," said Mother. "Only thank goodness I had mine taken out when I was a girl."

Dr. Burton agreed to do the job in front of a movie camera.

"I'll save you for the last, Old Pioneer," he told Dad. "The best for the last. Since the first day I laid eyes on your great, big, beautiful tonsils, I knew I wouldn't be content until I got my hands on them."

"Stop drooling and put away your scalpel, you old flatterer you," said Dad. "I intend to be the last. I'll have mine out after the kids get better."

Dr. Burton said he would start with Anne and go right down the ladder, through Ernestine, Frank, Bill and Lillian.

Martha alone of the older children didn't need to have her tonsils out, the doctor said, and the children younger than Lillian could wait awhile.

The night before the mass operation, Martha was told she would sleep at the house of Dad's oldest sister, Aunt Anne.

"I don't want you underfoot," Dad informed her. "The children who are going to have their tonsils out won't be able to have any supper tonight or breakfast in the morning. I don't want you around to lord it over them."

Martha hadn't forgotten how we neglected her when she finally came down with the measles. She lorded it over us plenty before she finally departed.

"Aunt Anne always has apple pie for breakfast," she said, which we all knew to be perfectly true, except that sometimes it was blueberry instead of apple. "She keeps a jar of doughnuts in the pantry and she likes children to eat them." This, too, was unfortunately no more than the simple truth. "Tomorrow morning, when you are awaiting the knife, I will be thinking of you. I shall try, if I am not too full, to dedicate a doughnut to each of you."

She rubbed her stomach with a circular motion, and puffed out her cheeks horribly as if she were chewing on a whole doughnut.

She opened an imaginary doughnut jar and helped herself to another, which she rammed into her mouth.

"My goodness, Aunt Anne," she said, pretending that that lady was in the room, "those doughnuts are even more delicious than usual." . . . "Well, why don't you have another, Martha?" . . . "Thanks, Aunt Anne, I believe I will." . . . "Why don't you take two or three, Martha?" . . . "I'm so full of apple pie I don't know whether I could eat two more, Aunt Anne. But since it makes you happy to have people eat your cooking, I will do my best."

"Hope you choke, Martha, dear," we told her.

The next morning, the five of us selected to give our tonsils for motion study assembled in the parlor. As Martha had predicted, our stomachs were empty. They growled and rumbled. We could hear beds being moved around upstairs, and we knew the wards were being set up again. In the laboratory, which adjoined the parlor, Dad, his movie cameraman, a nurse, and Dr. Burton were converting a desk into an operating table, and setting up the cross-section background and lights.

Dad came into the parlor, dressed like an Alp again. "All right, Anne, come on." He thumped her on the back and smiled at the rest of us. "There's nothing to it. It will be over in just a few minutes. And think of the fun we'll have looking at the movies and seeing how each of you looks when he's asleep."

As he and Anne went out, we could see that his hands were trembling. Sweat was beginning to pop through his white robe. Mother came in and sat with us. Dad had wanted her to watch the operations, but she said she couldn't. After awhile we heard Dad and a nurse walking heavily up the front stairs, and we knew Anne's operation was over and she was being carried to bed.

"I know I'm next, and I won't say I'm not scared," Ernestine confided. "But I'm so hungry all I can think of is Martha and that pie. The lucky dog."

"And doughnuts," said Bill. "The lucky dog."

"Can we have pie and doughnuts after our operations?" Lill asked Mother.

"If you want them," said Mother, who had had her tonsils out.

Dad came into the room. His robe was dripping sweat now. It looked as if a spring thaw had come to the Alps.

"Nothing to it," he said. "And I know we got some great movies. Anne slept just like a baby. All right, Ernestine, girl. You're next; let's go."

"I'm not hungry any more," she said. "Now I'm just scared."

A nurse put a napkin saturated with ether over Ern's nose. The last thing she remembered was Mr. Coggin, Dad's photographer, grinding away at the camera. "He should be cranking at two revolutions a second," she thought. "I'll count and see if he is. And one and two and three and four. That's the way Dad says to count seconds. You have to put the 'and' in between the numbers to count at the right speed. And one and two and three . . ." She fell asleep.

Dr. Burton peered into her mouth.

"My God, Gilbreth," he said. "I told you I didn't want Martha."

"You haven't got Martha," Dad said. "That's Ernestine."

"Are you sure?"

"Of course I'm sure, you jackass. Don't you think I know my own children?"

"You must be mistaken," Dr. Burton insisted. "Look at her carefully. There, now, isn't that Martha?"

"You mean to say you think I can't tell one child from another?"

"I don't mean to say anything, except if that isn't Martha we've made a horrible mistake."

"We?" Dad squealed. "We? I've made no mistake. And I hope I'm wrong in imagining the sort of a mistake you've made."

"You see, all I know them by is their tonsils," said Dr. Burton. "I thought these tonsils were Martha. They were the only pair that didn't have to come out."

"No," moaned Dad. "Oh, no!" Then growing indignant: "Do you mean to tell me you knocked my little girl unconscious for no reason at all?"

"It looks as if I did just that, Gilbreth. I'm sorry, but it's done. It was damned careless. But you do have an uncommon lot of them, and they all look just alike to me."

"All right, Burton," Dad said. "Sorry I lost my temper. What do we do?"

"I'm going to take them out anyway. They'd have to come out eventually at any rate, and the worst part of an operation is dreading it before hand. She's done her dreading, and there's no use to make her do it twice."

As Dr. Burton leaned over Ernestine, some reflex caused her to knee him in the mouth.

"Okay, Ernestine, if that's really your name," he muttered. "I guess I deserved that."

As it turned out, Ernestine's tonsils were recessed and bigger than the doctor had expected. It was a little messy to get at them, and Mr. Coggin, the movie cameraman, was sick in a waste basket.

"Don't stop cranking," Dad shouted at him, "or your tonsils will be next. I'll pull them out by the roots, myself. Crank, by jingo, crank."

Mr. Coggin cranked. When the operation was over, Dad and the nurse carried Ernestine upstairs.

When Dad came in the parlor to get Frank, he told Mother to send someone over to Aunt Anne's for Martha.

"Apple pie, doughnuts or not, she's going to have her tonsils out," he said. "I'm not going to go through another day like this one again in a hurry."

Frank, Bill, and Lillian had their tonsils out, in that order. Then Martha arrived, bawling, kicking, and full of pie and doughnuts.

"You said I didn't have to have my tonsils out, and I'm not going to have my tonsils out," she screamed at the doctor. Before he could get her on the desk which served as the operating table, she kicked him in the stomach.

"The next time I come to your house," he said to Dad as soon as he could get his breath, "I'm going to wear a chest protector and a catcher's mask." Then to the nurse: "Give some ether to Martha, if that's really her name."

"Yes, I'm Martha," she yelled through the towel. "You're making a mistake."

"I told you she was Martha," Dad said triumphantly.

"I know," Dr. Burton said. "Let's not go into that again. She's Martha, but I've named her tonsils Ernestine. Open your mouth, Martha, you sweet child, and let me get Ernestine's tonsils. Crank on Mr. Coggin. Your film may be the first photographic record of a man slowly going berserk."

All of us felt terribly sick that afternoon, but Martha was in agony.

"It's a shame," Grandma kept telling Martha, who was named for her and was her especial pet. "They shouldn't have let you eat all that stuff and then brought you back here for the butchering. I don't care whether it was the doctor's fault or your father's fault. I'd like to skin them both alive and then scalp them like red Indians."

While we were recuperating, Dad spent considerable time with us, but minimized our discomforts, and kept telling us we were just looking for sympathy.

"Don't tell me," he said. "I saw the operations, didn't I? Why there's only the little, tiniest cut at the back of your throat. I don't understand how you can do all that complaining. Don't you remember the story about the Spartan boy who kept his mouth shut while the fox was chewing on his vitals?"

It was partly because of our complaining, and the desire to show us how the Spartan boy would have had his tonsils out, that Dad decided to have only a local anesthetic for his operation. Mother, Grandma, and Dr. Burton all advised against it. But Dad wouldn't listen.

"Why does everyone want to make a mountain out of a molehill over such a minor operation?" he said. "I want to keep an eye on Burton and see that he doesn't mess up the job."

The first day that we children were well enough to get up, Dad and Mother set out in the car for Dr. Burton's office. Mother had urged Dad to call a taxi. She didn't know how to drive, and she said Dad probably wouldn't feel like doing the driving on the way home. But Dad laughed at her qualms.

"We'll be back in about an hour," Dad called to us as he tested his three horns to make sure he was prepared for any emergency. "Wait lunch for us. I'm starving."

"You've got to hand it to him," Anne admitted as the Pierce Arrow bucked up Wayside Place. "He's the bee's knees, all right.

We were all scared to death before our operations. And look at him. He's looking forward to it."

Two hours later, a taxicab stopped in front of the house, and the driver jumped out and opened the door for his passengers. Then Mother emerged, pale and red-eyed. She and the driver helped a crumpled mass of moaning blue serge to alight. Dad's hat was rumpled and on sideways. His face was gray and sagging. He wasn't crying, but his eyes were watering. He couldn't speak and he couldn't smile.

"He's sure got a load on all right, Mrs. Gilbreth," said the driver enviously. "And still early afternoon, too. Didn't even know he touched the stuff, myself."

We waited for the lightning to strike, but it didn't. The seriousness of Dad's condition may be adjudged by the fact that he contented himself with a withering look.

"Keep a civil tongue in your head," said Mother, in one of the sharpest speeches of her career. "He's deathly ill."

Mother and Grandma helped Dad up to his room. We could hear him moaning, all the way downstairs.

Mother told us all about it that night, while Dad was snoring under the effects of sleeping pills. Mother had waited in Dr. Burton's ante-room while the tonsillectomy was being performed. Dad had felt wonderful while under the local anesthetic. When the operation was half over, he had come out into the ante-room, grinning and waving one tonsil in a pair of forceps.

"One down and one to go, Lillie," he had said. "Completely painless. Just like rolling off a log."

After what had seemed an interminable time, Dad had come out into the waiting room again, and reached for his hat and coat. He was still grinning, only not so wide as before.

"That's that," he said. "Almost painless. All right, boss, let's go. I'm still hungry."

Then, as Mother watched, his high spirits faded and he began to fall to pieces.

"I'm stabbed," he moaned. "I'm hemorrhaging. Burton, come here. Quick. What have you done to me?"

Dr. Burton came out of his office. It must be said to his credit that he was sincerely sympathetic. Dr. Burton had had his own tonsils out.

"You'll be all right, Old Pioneer," he said. "You just had to have it the hard way."

Dad obviously couldn't drive, so Mother had called the taxi. A man from the garage towed Foolish Carriage home later that night.

"I tried to drive it home," the garage man told Mother, "but I couldn't budge it. I got the engine running all right, but it just spit and bucked every time I put it in gear. Durndest thing I ever saw."

"I don't think anyone but Mr. Gilbreth understands it," Mother said.

Dad spent two weeks in bed, and it was the first time any of us remembered his being sick. He couldn't smoke, eat, or talk. But he could glare, and he glared at Bill for two full minutes when Bill asked him one afternoon if he had had his tonsils taken out like the Spartans used to have theirs removed.

Dad didn't get his voice back until the very day that he finally got out of bed. He was lying there, propped up on pillows, reading his office mail. There was a card from Mr. Coggin, the photographer.

"Hate to tell you, Mr. Gilbreth. but none of the moving pictures came out. I forgot to take off the inside lens cap. I'm terribly sorry. Coggin. P.S. I quit."

Dad threw off the covers and reached for his bathrobe. For the first time in two weeks, he spoke:

"I'll track him down to the ends of the earth," he croaked. "I'll take a blunt button hook and pull his tonsils out by the by jingoed roots, just like I promised him. He doesn't quit. He's fired."

CHAPTER 11

Nantucket

WE spent our summers at Nantucket, Massachusetts, where Dad bought two lighthouses, which had been abandoned by the government, and a ramshackle cottage, which looked as if it had been abandoned by Coxey's Army. Dad had the lighthouses moved so that they flanked the cottage. He and Mother used one of them as an office and den. The other served as a bedroom for three of the children.

He named the cottage *The Shoe*, in honor of Mother, who, he said, reminded him of the old woman who lived in one.

The cottage and lighthouses were situated on a flat stretch of land between the fashionable Cliff and the Bathing Beach. Besides our place, there was only one other house in the vicinity. This belonged to an artist couple named Whitney. But after our first summer at Nantucket, the Whitneys had their house jacked up,

114

placed on rollers, and moved a mile away to a vacant lot near the tip of Brant Point. After that, we had the strip of land all to ourselves.

Customarily, en route from Montclair to Nantucket, we spent the night in a hotel in New London, Connecticut. Dad knew the hotel manager and all of the men at the desk, and they used to exchange loud and good-natured insults for the benefit of the crowds that followed us in from the street.

"Oh, Lord, look what's coming," the manager called when we entered the door. And then to an assistant. "Alert the fire depart-ment and the house detective. It's the Gilbreths. And take that cigar cutter off the counter and lock it in the safe."

"Do you still have that dangerous guillotine?" Dad grinned. "I know you'll be disappointed to hear that the finger grew in just as good as new. Show the man your finger, Ernestine."

Ernestine held up the little finger of her right hand. On a previous visit, she had pushed it inquisitively into the cigar cutter, and had lost about an eighth of an inch of it. She had bled considerably on a rug, while Dad tried to fashion a tourniquet and roared inquiries about whether there was a doctor in the house.

"Tell me," Dad remarked as he picked up a pen to register in the big book, "do my Irishmen come cheaper by the dozen?"

"Irishmen! If I were wearing a sheet, you'd call them Arabs. How many of them are there, anyway? Last year, when I went to make out your bill, you claimed there were only seven. I can count at least a dozen of them now."

"It's quite possible there may have been some additions since then," Dad conceded.

"Front, boy. Front, boy. Front, boy. Front, boy. You four boys show Mr. and Mrs. Gilbreth and their seven—or so—Irishmen to 503, 504, 505, 506, and 507. And mind you take good care of them, too."

When we first started going to Nantucket, which is off the tip of Cape Cod, automobiles weren't allowed on the island, and we'd leave the Pierce Arrow in a garage at New Bedford, Massachusetts. Later, when the automobile ban was lifted, we'd take the car with us on the *Gay Head* or the *Sankaty*, the steamers which plied between the mainland and the island. Dad had a frightening time backing the automobile up the gangplank. Mother insisted that we get out of the car and stand clear. Then she'd beg Dad to put on a life preserver.

"I know you and it are going into the water one of these days," she warned.

"Doesn't anybody, even my wife, have confidence in my driving?" he would moan. Then on a more practical note. "Besides, I can swim."

The biggest problem, on the boat and in the car, was Martha's two canaries, which she had won for making the best recitation in Sunday school. All of us, except Dad, were fond of them. Dad called one of them Shut Up and the other You Heard Me. He said they smelled so much that they ruined his whole trip, and were the only creatures on earth with voices louder than his children. Tom Grieves, the handyman, who had to clean up the cage, named the birds Peter Soil and Maggie Mess. Mother wouldn't let us use those full names; she said they were "Eskimo." (Eskimo was Mother's description of anything that was off-color, revolting, or evil-minded.) We called the birds simply Peter and Maggie.

On one trip, Fred was holding the cage on the stern of the ship, while Dad backed the car aboard. Somehow, the wire door popped open and the birds escaped. They flew to a piling on the dock, and then to a roof of a warehouse. When Dad, with the car finally stowed away, appeared on deck, three of the younger children were sobbing. They made so much noise that the captain heard them and came off the bridge.

"What's the trouble now, Mr. Gilbreth?" he asked.

"Nothing," said Dad, who saw a chance to put thirty miles between himself and the canaries. "You can shove off at any time, captain."

"No one tells me when to shove off until I'm ready to shove off," the captain announced stubbornly. He leaned over Fred. "What's the matter, son?"

"Peter and Maggie," bawled Fred. "They've gone over the rail."

"My God," the captain blanched. "I've been afraid this would happen ever since you Gilbreths started coming to Nantucket."

"Peter and Maggie aren't Gilbreths," Dad said irritatedly. "Why don't you just forget about the whole thing and shove off?"

The captain leaned over Fred again. "Peter and Maggie who? Speak up, boy!"

Fred stopped crying. "I'm not allowed to tell you their last names," he said. "Mother says they're Eskimo."

The captain was bewildered. "I wish someone would make sense," he complained. "You say Peter and Maggie, the Eskimos, have disappeared over the rail?"

Fred nodded. Dad pointed to the empty cage. "Two canaries," Dad shouted, "known as Peter and Maggie and by other aliases, have flown the coop. No matter. We wouldn't think of delaying you further."

"Where did they fly to, sonny?"

Fred pointed to the roof of the warehouse. The captain sighed.

"I can't stand to see children cry," he said. He walked back to the bridge and started giving orders.

Four crew members, armed with crab nets, climbed to the roof of the warehouse. While passengers shouted encouragement from the rail, the men chased the birds across the roof, back to the dock, onto the rigging of the ship, and back to the warehouse again. Finally Peter and Maggie disappeared altogether, and the captain had to give up.

"I'm sorry, Mr. Gilbreth," he said. "I guess we'll have to shove off without your canaries."

"You've been too kind already," Dad beamed.

Dad felt good for the rest of the trip, and even managed to convince Martha of the wisdom of throwing the empty, but still smelly, bird cage over the side of the ship.

The next day, after we settled in our cottage, a cardboard box arrived from the captain. It was addressed to Fred, and it had holes punched in the top.

"You don't have to tell *me* what's in it," Dad said glumly. "I've got a nose." He reached in his wallet and handed Martha a bill. "Take this and go down to the village and buy another cage. And after this, I hope you'll be more careful of your belongings."

Our cottage had one small lavatory, but no hot water, shower, or bathtub. Dad thought that living a primitive life in the summer was healthful. He also believed that cleanliness was next to godliness, and as a result all of us had to go swimming at least once a day. The rule was never waived, even when the temperature dropped to the fifties, and a cold, gray rain was falling. Dad would lead the way from the house to the beach, dog-trotting, holding a bar of soap in one hand, and beating his chest with the other.

"Look out, ocean, here comes a tidal wave. Brrr. Last one in is Kaiser Bill."

Then he'd take a running dive and disappear in a geyser of spray. He'd swim under water a ways, allow his feet to emerge, wiggle his toes, swim under water some more, and then come up head first, grinning and spitting a thin stream of water through his teeth.

"Come on," he'd call. "It's wonderful once you get in." And he'd start lathering himself with soap.

Mother was the only non-swimmer, except the babies. She hated cold water, she hated salt water, and she hated bathing suits. Bathing suits itched her, and although she wore the most conservative models, with long sleeves and black stockings, she never felt modest in them. Dad used to say Mother put on more clothes than she took off when she went swimming.

Mother's swims consisted of testing the water with the tip of a black bathing shoe, wading cautiously out to her knees, making some tentative dabs in the water with her hands, splashing a few drops on her shoulders, and, finally, in a moment of supreme courage, pinching her nose and squatting down until the water reached her chest. The nose-pinch was an unnecessary precaution, because her nose never came within a foot of the water.

Then, with teeth chattering, she'd hurry back to the house, where she'd take a cold water sponge bath, to get rid of the salt.

"My, the water was delightful this morning, wasn't it?" she'd say brightly at the lunch table.

"I've seen fish who found the air more delightful than you do the water," Dad would remark.

As in every other phase of teaching, Dad knew his business as a swimming instructor. Some of us learned to swim when we were as young as three years old, and all of us had learned by the time we were five. It was a sore point with Dad that Mother was the only pupil he ever had encountered with whom he had no success.

"This summer," he'd tell Mother at the start of every vacation, "I'm really going to teach you, if it's the last thing I do. It's dangerous not to know how to swim. What would you do if you were on a boat that sank? Leave me with a dozen children on my hands, I suppose! After all, you should have some consideration for me."

"I'll try again," Mother said patiently. But you could tell she knew it was hopeless.

Once they had gone down to the beach, Dad would take her hand and lead her. Mother would start out bravely enough, but would begin holding back about the time the water got to her knees. We'd form a ring around her and offer her what encouragement we could.

"That's the girl, Mother," we'd say. "It's not going to hurt you. Look at me. Look at me."

"Please don't splash," Mother would say. "You know how I hate to be splashed."

"For Lord's sakes, Lillie," said Dad. "Come out deeper."

"Isn't this deep enough?"

"You can't learn to swim if you're hard aground."

"No matter how deep we go, I always end up aground anyway."

"Don't be scared, now. Come on. This time it will be different. You'll see."

Dad towed her out until the water was just above her waist. "Now the first thing you have to do," he said, "is to learn the dead man's float. If a dead man can do it, so can you."

"I don't even like its name. It sounds ominous."

"Like this, Mother. Look at me."

"You kids clear out," said Dad. "But, Lillie, if the children can do it, you, a grown woman, should be able to. Come on now. You can't help but float, because the human body, when inflated with air, is lighter than water."

"You know I always sink."

"That was last year. Try it now. Be a sport. I won't let anything happen to you."

"I don't want to."

"You don't want to show the white feather in front of all the kids."

"I don't care if I show the whole albatross," Mother said. "But I don't suppose I'll have another minute's peace until I try it. So here goes. And remember, I'm counting on you not to let anything happen to me."

"You'll float. Don't worry."

Mother took a deep breath, stretched herself out on the surface, and sank like a stone. Dad waited a while, still convinced that under the laws of physics she must ultimately rise. When she didn't, he finally reached down in disgust and fished her up. Mother was gagging, choking up water, and furious.

"See what I mean?" she finally managed.

Dad was furious, too. "Are you sure you didn't do that on purpose?" he asked her.

"Mercy, Maud," Mother sputtered. "Mercy, mercy, Maud. Do you think I like it down there in Davey Jones' locker?"

"Davey Jones' locker," scoffed Dad. "Why you weren't even four feet under water. You weren't even in his attic."

"Well, it seemed like his locker to me. And I'm never going down there again. You ought to be convinced by now that Archimedes' principle simply doesn't apply, so far as I am concerned."

Coughing and blowing her nose, Mother started for the beach.

"I still don't understand it," Dad muttered. "She's right. It completely refutes Archimedes."

Dad had promised before we came to Nantucket that there would be no formal studying—no language records and no school books. He kept his promise, although we found he was always teaching us things informally, when our backs were turned.

For instance, there was the matter of the Morse code.

"I have a way to teach you the code without any studying," he announced one day at lunch.

We said we didn't want to learn the code, that we didn't want to learn anything until school started in the fall.

"There's no studying," said Dad, "and the ones who learn it first will get rewards. The ones who don't learn it are going to wish they had."

After lunch, he got a small paint brush and a can of black enamel, and locked himself in the lavatory, where he painted the alphabet in code on the wall.

For the next three days Dad was busy with his paint brush, writing code over the whitewash in every room in *The Shoe*. On the ceiling in the dormitory bedrooms, he wrote the alphabet together with key words, whose accents were a reminder of the code for the various letters. It went like this: A, dot-dash, a-BOUT; B, dash-dot-dot-dot, BOIS-ter-ous-ly; C, dash-dot-dash-dot, CARE-less CHILD-ren; D, dash-dot-dot, DAN-ger-ous, etc.

When you lay on your back, dozing, the words kept going through your head, and you'd find yourself saying, "DAN-ger-ous, dash-dot-dot, DAN-ger-ous."

He painted secret messages in code on the walls of the front porch and dining room.

"What do they say, Daddy?" we asked him.

"Many things," he replied mysteriously. "Many secret things and many things of great humor."

We went into the bedrooms and copied the code alphabet on pieces of paper. Then, referring to the paper, we started translating Dad's messages. He went right on painting, as if he were paying no attention to us, but he didn't miss a word.

"Lord, what awful puns," said Anne. "And this, I presume, is meant to fit into the category of 'things of great humor.' Listen to this one: 'Bee it ever so bumble there's no place like comb.'"

"And we're stung," Ern moaned. "We're not going to be satisfied until we translate them all. I see dash-dot-dash-dot, and I hear myself repeating CARE-less CHILD-ren. What's this one say?"

We figured it out: "When igorots is bliss, 'tis folly to be white." And another, by courtesy of Mr. Irvin S. Cobb, "Eat, drink and be merry for tomorrow you may diet." And still another, which Mother made Dad paint out, "Two maggots were fighting in dead Ernest."

"That one is Eskimo," said Mother. "I won't have it in my dining room, even in Morse code."

"All right, boss," Dad grinned sheepishly. "I'll paint over it. It's already served its purpose, anyway."

Every day or so after that, Dad would leave a piece of paper, containing a Morse code message, on the dining room table. Translated, it might read something like this: "The first one who figures out this secret message should look in the right hand pocket of my linen knickers, hanging on a hook in my room. Daddy." Or: "Hurry up before someone beats you to it, and look in the bottom, left drawer of the sewing machine."

In the knickers' pocket and in the drawer would be some sort of reward—a Hershey bar, a quarter, a receipt entitling the bearer to one chocolate ice cream soda at Coffin's Drug Store, payable by Dad on demand.

Some of the Morse code notes were false alarms. "Hello, Live Bait. This one is on the house. No reward. But there may be a reward next time. When you finish reading this, dash off like mad so the next fellow will think you are on some hot clue. Then he'll read it, too, and you won't be the only one who got fooled. Daddy."

As Dad had planned, we all knew the Morse code fairly well within a few weeks. Well enough, in fact, so that we could tap out messages to each other by bouncing the tip of a fork on a butter plate. When a dozen or so persons all attempt to broadcast in this manner, and all of us preferred sending to receiving, the accumulation is loud and nerve-shattering. A present-day equivalent might be reproduced if the sound-effects man on *Gangbusters* and Walter Winchell should go on the air simultaneously, before a battery of powerful amplifiers.

The wall-writing worked so well in teaching us the code that Dad decided to use the same system to teach us astronomy. His first step was to capture our interest, and he did this by fashioning a telescope from a camera tripod and a pair of binoculars. He'd tote the contraption out into the yard on clear nights, and look at the stars, while apparently ignoring us.

We'd gather around and nudge him, and pull at his clothes, demanding that he let us look through the telescope.

"Don't bother me," he'd say, with his nose stuck into the glasses. "Oh, my golly, I believe those two stars are going to collide! No. Awfully close, though. Now I've got to see what the Old Beetle's up to. What a star, what a star!"

"Daddy, give us a turn," we'd insist. "Don't be a pig."

Finally, with assumed reluctance, he agreed to let us look through the glasses. We could see the ring on Saturn, three moons on Jupiter, and the craters on our own moon. Dad's favorite star was Betelgeuse, the yellowish red "Old Beetle" in the Orion constellation. He took a personal interest in her, because some of his friends were collaborating in experiments to measure her diameter by Michelson's interferometer.

When he finally was convinced he had interested us in astronomy, Dad started a new series of wall paintings dealing with stars. On one wall he made a scale drawing of the major planets, ranging from little Mercury, represented by a circle about as big as a marble, to Jupiter, as big as a basketball. On another, he showed the planets in relation to their distances from the sun, with Mercury the closest and Neptune the farthest away—almost in the kitchen. Pluto still hadn't been discovered, which was just as well, because there really wasn't room for it.

Dr. Harlow Shapley of Harvard gave Dad a hundred or more

photographs of stars, nebulae and solar eclipses. Dad hung these on the wall, near the floor. He explained that if they were up any higher, at the conventional level for pictures, the smaller children wouldn't be able to see them.

There was still some wall space left, and Dad had more than enough ideas to fill it. He tacked up a piece of cross-section graph paper, which was a thousand lines long and a thousand lines wide, and thus contained exactly a million little squares.

"You hear people talk a lot about a million," he said, "but not many people have ever seen exactly a million things at the same time. If a man has a million dollars, he has exactly as many dollars as there are little squares on that chart."

"Do you have a million dollars, Daddy?" Bill asked.

"No," said Dad a little ruefully. "I have a million children, instead. Somewhere along the line, a man has to choose between the two."

He painted diagrams in the dining room showing the difference between meters and feet, kilograms and pounds, liters and quarts. And he painted seventeen mysterious-looking symbols, representing each of the Therbligs, on a wall near the front door.

The Therbligs were discovered, or maybe a better word would be diagnosed, by Dad and Mother. Everybody has seventeen of them, they said, and the Therbligs can be used in such a way as to make life difficult or easy for their possessor.

A lazy man, Dad believed, always makes the best use of his Therbligs because he is too indolent to waste motions. Whenever Dad started to do a new motion study project at a factory, he'd always begin by announcing he wanted to photograph the motions of the laziest man on the job.

"The kind of fellow I want," he'd say, "is the fellow who is so lazy he won't even scratch himself. You must have one of those around some place. Every factory has them."

Dad named the Therbligs for himself—Gilbreth spelled backwards, with a slight variation. They were the basic theorems of his business and resulted indirectly in such things as foot levers to open garbage cans, special chairs for factory workers, redesign of typewriters, and some aspects of the assembly line technique.

Using Therbligs, Dad had shown Regal Shoe Company clerks how they could take a customer's shoe off in seven seconds, and put it back on again and lace it up in twenty-two seconds.

Actually, a Therblig is a unit of motion or thought. Suppose a man goes into the bathroom to shave. We'll assume that his face is all lathered and he is ready to pick up his razor. He knows where the razor is, but first he must locate it with his eye. That is "search," the first Therblig. His eye finds it and comes to rest— that's "find," the second Therblig. Third comes "select," the process of sliding the razor prior to the fourth Therblig, "grasp." Fifth is "transport loaded," bringing the razor up to the face, and sixth is "position," getting the razor set on the face. There are eleven other Therbligs—the last one is "think!"

When Dad made a motion study, he broke down each operation into a Therblig, and then tried to reduce the time taken to perform each Therblig. Perhaps certain parts to be assembled could be painted red and others green, so as to reduce the time required for "search" and "find." Perhaps the parts could be moved closer to the object being assembled, so as to reduce the time required for "transport loaded."

Every Therblig had its own symbol, and once they were painted on the wall Dad had us apply them to our household chores—bed-making, dish-washing, sweeping, and dusting.

Meanwhile, *The Shoe* and the lighthouses had become a stop on some of the Nantucket sightseeing tours. The stop didn't entail getting out of the carriages or, later, the buses. But we'd hear the drivers giving lurid and inaccurate accounts of the history of the place and the family which inhabited it. Some individuals occasionally would come up to the door and ask if they could peek in, and if the house was presentable we'd usually show them around.

Then, unexpectedly, the names of strangers started appearing in a guest book which we kept in the front room.

"Are these friends of yours?" Dad asked Mother.

"I never heard of them before. Maybe they're friends of the children."

When we said we didn't know them, Dad questioned Tom Grieves, who admitted readily enough that he had been showing tourists through the house and lighthouses, while we were at the beach. Tom's tour included the dormitories; Mother's and Dad's room, where the baby stayed; and even the lavatory, where he pointed out the code alphabet. Some of the visitors, seeing the guest book on the table, thought they were supposed to sign. Tom stood at the front door as the tourists filed out, and frequently collected tips.

Mother was irked. "I never heard of such a thing in all my born days. Imagine taking perfect strangers through our bedrooms, and the house a wreck, most likely."

"Well," said Dad, who was convinced the tourists had come to see his visual education methods, "there's no need for us to be selfish about the ideas we've developed. Maybe it's not a bad plan to let the public see what we're doing."

He leaned back reflectively in his chair, an old mahogany pew from some church. Dad had found the pew, disassembled, in the basement of our cottage. He had resurrected it reverently, rubbed it down, put it together, and varnished it. The pew was his seat of authority in *The Shoe*, and the only chair which fitted him comfortably and in which he could place complete confidence.

"I wonder how much money Tom took in," he said to Mother. "Maybe we could work out some sort of an arrangement so that Tom could split tips from future admissions . . ."

"The idea!" said Mother. "There'll be no future admissions. The very idea."

"Can't you take a joke? I was only joking. Where's your sense of humor?"

"I know." Mother nodded her head. "I'm not supposed to have any. But did you ever stop to think that there might be some women, somewhere, who might think their husbands were joking if they said they had bought two lighthouses and . . ."

Dad started to laugh, and as he rocked back and forth he shook the house so that loose whitewash flaked off the ceiling and landed on the top of his head. When Dad laughed, everybody laughed—you couldn't help it. And Mother, after a losing battle to remain severe, joined in.

"By jingo," he wheezed. "And I guess there are some women, somewhere, who wouldn't want the Morse code, and planets, and even Therbligs, painted all over the walls of their house, either. Come over here, boss, and let me take back everything I ever said about your sense of humor."

Mother walked over and brushed the whitewash out of what was left of his hair.

The Rena

DAD acquired the *Rena* to reward us for learning to swim. She was a catboat, twenty feet long and almost as wide. She was docile, dignified, and ancient.

Before we were allowed aboard the *Rena*, Dad delivered a series of lectures about navigation, tides, the magnetic compass, seamanship, rope-splicing, right-of-way, and nautical terminology. Radar still had not been invented. It is doubtful if, outside the Naval Academy at Annapolis, any group of Americans ever received a more thorough indoctrination before setting foot on a catboat.

Next followed a series of dry runs, on the front porch of *The Shoe*. Dad, sitting in a chair and holding a walking stick as if it were a tiller, would bark out orders while maneuvering his imaginary craft around a tricky harbor.

We'd sit in line on the floor along side of him, pretending we were holding down the windward rail. Dad would rub imaginary spray out of his eyes, and scan the horizon for possible sperm whale, Flying Dutchmen, or floating ambergris.

"Great Point Light off the larboard bow," he'd bark. "Haul in the sheet and we'll try to clear her on this tack."

He'd ease the handle of the cane over toward the imaginary lee-ward rail, and two of us would haul in an imaginary rope.

"Steady as she goes," Dad would command. "Make her fast."

We'd make believe twist the rope around a cleet.

"Coming about," he'd shout. "Low bridge. Ready about, hard a'lee."

This time he'd push the cane handle all the way over toward the leeward side. We'd duck our heads and then scramble across the porch to man the opposite rail.

"Now we'll come up and pick up our mooring. You do that at the end of every sail. Good sailors always make the mooring on the first try. Landlubbers sometimes have to go around three or four times before they can catch it."

He'd stand up in the stern, the better to squint at the imaginary mooring.

"Now. Let go your sheet, Bill. Stand by the centerboard, Mart. Up on the bow with the boat hook, Anne and Ernestine, and mind you grab that mooring. Stand by the throat, Frank. Stand by the peak, Fred. . . ."

We'd scurry around the porch going through our duties, until at last Dad was satisfied his new crew was ready for the high seas.

Dad was never happier than when aboard the *Rena*. From the moment he climbed into our dory to row out to *Rena's* mooring, his personality changed. On the *Rena*, we were no longer his flesh and blood, but a crew of landlubberly scum shanghaied from the taverns and fleshpots of many exotic ports. *Rena* was no scow-like catboat, but a sleek four-master, bound around the Horn with a bone in her teeth in search of rare spices and the priceless treasure of the Indies. He insisted that we address him as Captain, instead of Daddy, and every remark must needs be civil and end with a "sir."

"It's just like when he was in the Army," Ernestine whispered. "Remember those military haircuts for Frank and Bill, and all that business of snapping to attention and learning to salute, and the kitchen police?"

"Avast there, you swabs," Dad hollered. "No mutinous whispering on the poop deck!"

Anne, being the oldest, was proclaimed first mate of the *Rena.* Ernestine was second mate, Martha third, and Frank fourth. All the younger children were able-bodied seamen who, presumably, ate hardtack and bunked before the mast.

"Seems to be blowing up, mister," Dad said to Anne. "I'll have a reef in that mains'il."

"Aye, aye, sir."

"The *Rena's* just got one sail, Daddy," Lill said. "Is that the mains'il?"

"Quiet, you landlubber, or you'll get the merrie rope's end. Of course it's the mains'il."

The merrie rope's end was no idle threat. Able-bodied seamen or mates who failed to leap when Dad barked an order did in fact receive a flogging with a piece of rope. It hurt, too.

Dad's mood was contagious, and soon the mates were as dogmatic and as full of invective as he, when dealing with the sneaking pickpockets and rum-palsied derelicts who were their subordinates. And, somehow, Dad passed along to us the illusion that placid old *Rena* was a taunt ship.

"I'll have those halliards coiled," he told Anne.

"Aye, aye, sir. Come on you swabs. Look alive now, or shiver my timbers if I don't keel haul the lot of you."

Sometimes, without warning, Dad would start to bellow out tuneless chanties about the fifteen men on a dead man's chest and, especially, one that went, "He said heave her to, she replied make it three."

If there had been any irons aboard, they would have been occupied by the fumbling landlubber or scurvy swab who forgot his duties and made Dad miss the mooring. Dad felt that to have to make a second try for the mooring was the supreme humiliation, and that fellow yachtsmen and professional sea captains all along the waterfront were splitting their sides laughing at him. He'd drop the tiller, grow red in the face, and advance rope in hand on the offender. More than once, the scurvy swab made a panic-stricken dive over the side, preferring to swim ashore, where he would cope ultimately with Dad, instead of meeting the captain on the latter's own quarterdeck.

On one occasion, when Dad blamed missing a mooring on general inefficiency and picked up a merrie rope's end to inflict merrie mass punishment, the entire crew leaped simultaneously over the side in an unrehearsed abandon-ship maneuver. Only the captain remained at the helm, from which vantage point he hurled threatening reminders about the danger of sharks and the penalties of mutiny. On that occasion, he brought *Rena* up to the mooring by himself, without any trouble, thus proving something we had long suspected—that he didn't really need our help at all, but enjoyed teaching us and having a crew to order around.

Through the years, old *Rena* remained phlegmatic, paying no apparent attention to the bedlam which had intruded into her twilight years. She was too old a seadog to learn new tricks.

Only once, just for a second, did she display any sign of temperament. It was after a long sail. A fog had come up, and *Rena* was as clammy as a shower curtain. We had missed the mooring on the first go-round, and the captain was in an ugly mood. We made the mooring all right on the second try. The captain, as was his custom, was standing in the stern, merrie rope in hand, shouting orders about lowering the sail. Just before the sail came down, a squall hit *Rena*, and she retaliated by whipping her boom savagely across the hull. The captain saw it coming, but didn't have time to duck. The boom caught him on the side of the head with a terrific clout, a blow hard enough to lift him off his feet and tumble him, stomach first, into the water.

The captain didn't come up for almost a minute. The crew, while losing little love for their captain, became frightened for their Daddy. We were just about to dive in after him when a pair of feet emerged from the water and the toes wiggled. We knew everything was all right then. The feet disappeared, and a few moments later Dad came up head first. His nose was bleeding, but he was grinning and didn't forget to spit the fine stream of water through his front teeth.

"The bird they call the elephant," he whispered weakly, and he was Dad then. But not for long. As soon as his head cleared and his strength came back, he was the captain again.

"All right, you red lobsters, avast there," he bellowed. "Throw your captain a line and help haul me aboard. Or, shiver my timbers, I'll take a belaying pin to the swab who lowered the boom on me."

CHAPTER 13

Have You Seen the Latest Model?

IT was an off year that didn't bring a new Gilbreth baby. Both Dad and Mother wanted a large family. And if it was Dad who set the actual target of an even dozen, Mother as readily agreed.

Dad mentioned the dozen figure for the first time on their wedding day. They had just boarded a train at Oakland, California, after the ceremony, and Mother was trying to appear blasé, as if she had been married for years. She might have gotten away with it, too, if Dad had not stage whispered when she took off her hat prior to sitting down:

"Good Lord, woman, why didn't you tell me your hair was red?"

The heads of leering, winking passengers craned around. Mother slid into the seat and wiggled into a corner, where she tried to hide behind a magazine. Dad sat down next to her. He didn't say any-

135

thing more until the train got underway and they could talk without being heard throughout the car.

"I shouldn't have done that," he whispered. "It's just—I'm so proud of you I want everyone to look at you, and to know you're my wife."

"That's all right, dear. I'm glad you're proud of me."

"We're going to have a wonderful life, Lillie. A wonderful life and a wonderful family. A great big family."

"We'll have children all over the house," Mother smiled. "From the basement to the attic."

"From the floorboards to the chandelier."

"When we go for our Sunday walk we'll look like Mr. and Mrs. Pied Piper."

"Mr. Piper, shake hands with Mrs. Piper. Mrs. Piper, meet Mr. Piper."

Mother put the magazine on the seat between her and Dad, and they held hands beneath it.

"How many would you say we should have, just an estimate?" Mother asked.

"Just as an estimate, many."

"Lots and lots."

"We'll sell out for an even dozen," said Dad. "No less. What do you say to that?"

"I say," said Mother, "a dozen would be just right. No less."

"That's the minimum."

"Boys or girls?"

"Well, boys would be fine," Dad whispered. "A dozen boys would be just right. But . . . well, girls would be all right too. Sure. I guess."

"I'd like to have half boys and half girls. Do you think it would be all right to have half girls?"

"If that's what you want," Dad said, "we'll plan it that way. Excuse me a minute while I make a note of it." He took out his memorandum book and solemnly wrote: "Don't forget to have six boys and six girls."

They had a dozen children, six boys and six girls, in seventeen years. Somewhat to Dad's disappointment, there were no twins or other multiple births. There was no doubt in his mind that the most efficient way to rear a large family would be to have one huge litter and get the whole business over with at one time.

It was a year or so after the wedding, when Mother was expecting her first baby, that Dad confided to her his secret conviction that all of their children would be girls.

"Would it make much difference to you?" Mother asked him.

"Would it make much difference?" Dad asked in amazement. "To have a dozen girls and not a single boy?" And then realizing that he might upset Mother, he added quickly: "No, of course not. Anything you decide to have will be just fine with me."

Dad's conviction that he would have no boys was based on a hunch that the Gilbreth Name, of which he was terribly proud, would cease to exist with him; that he was the last of the Gilbreths. Dad was the only surviving male of the entire branch of his family. There were two or three other Gilbreths in the country, but apparently they were no relation to Dad. The name Gilbreth, in the case of Dad's family, was a fairly recent corruption of Galbraith. A clerk of court, in a small town in Maine, had misspelled Galbraith on some legal document, and it had proved easier for Dad's grandfather to change his name to Gilbreth—

which was how the clerk had spelled it—than to change the document.

So when Anne was born, in New York, Dad was not in the least bit disappointed, because he had known all along she would be a girl. It is doubtful if any father ever was more insane about an offspring. It was just as well that Anne was a girl. If she had been a boy, Dad might have toppled completely off the deep end, and run amok with a kris in his teeth.

Dad had long held theories about babies and, with the arrival of Anne, he was anxious to put them to a test. He believed that children, like little monkeys, were born with certain instincts of self-preservation, but that the instincts vanished because babies were kept cooped up in a crib. He was convinced that babies started learning things from the very minute they were born, and that it was wrong to keep them in a nursery. He always forbade baby talk in the presence of Anne or any of his subsequent off-spring.

"The only reason a baby talks baby talk," he said, "is because that's all he's heard from grownups. Some children are almost full grown before they learn that the whole world doesn't speak baby talk."

He also thought that to feel secure and wanted in the family circle, a baby should be brought up at the side of its parents. He put Anne's bassinet on a desk in his and Mother's bedroom, and talked to her as if she were an adult, about concrete, and his new houseboat, and efficiency, and all the little sisters she was going to have.

The German nurse whom Dad had employed was scornful. "Why she can't understand a thing you say," the nurse told Dad.

"How do you know?" Dad demanded. "And I wish you'd speak

German, like I told you to do, when you talk in front of the baby. I want her to learn both languages."

"What does a two-week-old baby know about German?" said the nurse, shaking her head.

"Never mind that," Dad replied. "I hired you because you speak German, and I want you to speak it." He picked up Anne and held her on his shoulder. "Hang on now, Baby. Imagine you are a little monkey in a tree in the jungle. Hang on to save your life."

"Mind now," said the nurse. "She can't hang on to anything. She's only two weeks old. You'll drop her. Mind, now."

"I'm minding," Dad said irritably. "Of course she can't hang on, the way you and her mother coddle her and repress all her natural instincts. Show the nurse how you can hang on, Anne, baby."

Anne couldn't. Instead, she spit up some milk on Dad's shoulder.

"Now is that any way to behave?" he asked her. "I'm surprised at you. But that's all right, honey. I know it's not your fault. It's the way you've been all swaddled up around here. It's enough to turn anybody's stomach."

"You'd better give her to me for awhile," Mother said. "That's enough exercise for one day."

A week later, Dad talked Mother into letting him see whether new babies were born with a natural instinct to swim.

"When you throw little monkeys into a river, they just automatically swim. That's the way monkey mothers teach their young. I'll try out Anne in the bathtub. I won't let anything happen to her."

"Are you crazy or something," the nurse shouted. "Mrs. Gilbreth, you're not going to let him drown that child."

"Keep quiet and maybe you'll learn something," Dad told her.

Anne liked the big bathtub just fine. But she made no effort to swim and Dad finally had to admit that the experiment was a failure.

"Now if it had been a boy," he said darkly to the nurse, when Mother was out of hearing.

The desk on which Anne's bassinet rested was within reach of the bed and was piled high with notes, *Iron Age* magazines, and the galley proofs of a book Dad had just written on reinforced concrete. Mother utilized the "unavoidable delay" of her confinement to read the proofs. At night, when the light was out, Dad would reach over into the bassinet and stroke the baby's hand. And once Mother woke up in the middle of the night and saw him leaning over the bassinet and whispering distinctly:

"Is ou a ittle bitty baby? Is ou Daddy's ittle bitty girl?"

"What was that, dear?" said Mother, smiling into the sheet.

Dad cleared his throat. "Nothing. I was just telling this noisy, ill-behaved, ugly little devil that she is more trouble than a barrel of monkeys."

"And just as much fun?"

"Every bit."

Dad and Mother moved to another New York apartment on Riverside Drive, where Mary and Ernestine were born. Then the family moved to Plainfield, New Jersey, where Martha put in an appearance. With four girls, Dad was reconciled to his fate of being the Last of the Gilbreths. He was not bitter; merely resigned. He kept repeating that a dozen girls would suit him just fine, and he made hearty jokes about "my harem." When visitors came to call, Dad would introduce Anne, Mary and Ernestine. Then he'd get Martha out of her crib and bring her into the living room. "And this," he'd say, "is the latest model. Complete

with all the improvements. And don't think that's all; we're expecting the 1911 model some time next month."

Although Mother's condition made the announcement unnecessary, he came out with it anyway. He never understood why this embarrassed Mother.

"I just don't see why you mind," he'd tell her later. "It's something to be proud of."

"Well, of course it is. Maybe I'm old-fashioned, but it seems to me a mistake to proclaim it from the housetops, or confide it to comparative strangers, until the baby arrives."

Still, Mother knew very well that Dad had to talk about his children, the children who had already arrived and those who were expected.

In spite of Mother's protests, Dad decided that the fifth child would be named for her. Mother didn't like the name Lillian, and had refused to pass the name along to any of the first four girls.

"No nonsense, now," Dad said. "We're running low on names, and this one is going to be named for you. Whether you like it or not, I want a little Lillian."

"But it could be a boy, you know."

"Boys!" Dad grunted. "Who wants boys?"

"Sooner or later there'll be a boy," Mother said. "Look what happened in my family." Mother's mother had six girls before she produced a boy.

"Sure," sighed Dad, "but your father wasn't the Last of the Gilbreths."

When Dr. Hedges came out of Mother's bedroom and announced that Mother and the fifth baby were doing nicely, Dad told him that "The Latest Model" was to be named Lillian.

"I think that's nice," Dr. Hedges said sympathetically. "Real nice. Of course, the other boys in his class may tease him about having a girl's name, but . . ."

"Yes, that's true," said Dad. "I hadn't thought of . . ." He grabbed the doctor by the shoulders and shook him. "Other boys?" he shouted. "Did you say other boys? Boys?"

"I hate to disappoint you, Mr. Gilbreth," grinned Dr. Hedges. "Especially since you've been telling everyone how much you wanted a fifth girl for your harem. But this one . . ."

Dad pushed him out of the way and rushed into the bedroom, where his first son was sleeping in a by now battered bassinet, on a desk once again covered with galley proofs. Dad and Mother timed their books to coincide with Mother's annual intervals of unavoidable delay.

"Chip off the old block," Dad cooed into the bassinet. "Every inch a Gilbreth. Oh, Lillie, how did you ever manage to do it?"

"Do you think he's all right?" Mother whispered.

"He's one I think we'd better keep," said Dad. "Do you know something? I didn't come right out and say so before, because I didn't want to upset you, and I knew you were doing the best you could. But I really wanted a boy all the time. I was just trying to make you feel better when I said I wanted a fifth girl."

Mother managed to keep a straight face. "Mercy, Maud, you certainly had everybody fooled," she said. "I thought you'd be simply furious if little 'Lillian' turned out to be a boy. You seemed so set on naming this one for me. Are you sure you're not disappointed?"

"Gee whiz," was all Dad could manage.

"What should we name him?"

Dad wasn't listening. He was still leaning over the bassinet, cooing. There was little doubt in Mother's mind, anyway, about what the baby would be named, and Dad clinched the matter by the next remark which he addressed to the baby.

"I've got to leave you now for a few minutes, Mr. Frank Bunker Gilbreth, Junior," he said, rolling out the name and savoring its sound. "I've got to make a few telephone calls and send some wires. And I've got to get some toys suitable for a boy baby. All the toys we have around this house are girl baby toys. Behave yourself while I'm gone and take care of your mother. That's one of your jobs from now on." And over his shoulder to Mother, "I'll be back in a few minutes, Lillie."

"Farewell, Next to Last of the Gilbreths," Mother whispered. But Dad still wasn't listening. As he closed the door carefully, Mother heard him bellowing:

"Anne, Mary, Ernestine, Martha. Did you hear the news? It's a boy. Frank Bunker Gilbreth, Junior. How do you like the sound of that? Every inch a Gilbreth. Chip off the old block. Hello, central? Central? Long Distance, please. It's a boy."

Having fathered one son, Dad took it pretty much for granted that all the rest of his children would be boys.

"The first four were just practice," he'd say to Mother, while glaring with assumed ferocity at the girls. "Of course, I suppose we ought to keep them. They might come in handy some day to scrub the pots and pans and mend the socks of the men folk. But I don't see that we need any more of them."

The girls would rush at him and Dad would let them topple him over on the rug. Martha, using his vest pockets for fingerholds, would climb up on his stomach and the other three would tickle him so that Martha would be joggled up and down when he laughed.

Number Six was born in Providence, where the family had moved in 1912. As Dad had assumed, the new addition was a boy. He was named William for Mother's father and one of her brothers.

"Good work, Lillie," Dad told Mother. But this time there was no elaborate praise and his tone of voice indicated that Mother merely had done the sort of competent job that one might expect from a competent woman. "There's our first half-dozen."

And when his friends asked him whether the new baby was a boy or a girl, he replied matter of factly: "Oh, we had another boy."

Dad hadn't been there during the delivery. Both he and Mother agreed that it didn't help matters for him to be pacing up and down the hall, and Dad's business was placing more and more demands upon his time.

Mother had her first half-dozen babies at home, instead of in hospitals, because she liked to run the house and help Dad with his work, even during the confinements. She'd supervise the household right up until each baby started coming. There was a period of about twenty-four hours, then, when she wasn't much help to anybody. But she had prepared all the menus in advance, and the house ran smoothly by itself during the one day devoted to the delivery. For the next ten days to two weeks, while she remained in bed, we'd file in every morning so that she could tie the girls' hair ribbons and make sure the boys had washed properly. Then we'd come back again at night to hold the new baby and listen to Mother read *The Five Little Peppers*. Mother enjoyed the little Peppers every bit as much as we, and was particularly partial to a character named Phronsie, or something like that.

When Dad's mother came to live with us, Mother decided **to** have Number Seven in a Providence hospital, since Grandma could run the house for her. Six hours after Mother checked into the hospital, a nurse called our house and told Dad that Mrs. Gilbreth had had a nine-pound boy.

"Quick work," Dad told Grandma. "She really has found the one best way of having babies."

Grandma asked whether it was a boy or a girl, and Dad replied: "A boy, naturally, for goodness sakes. What did you expect?"

A few moments later, the hospital called again and said there had been some mistake. A Mrs. Gilbert, not Gilbreth, had had the baby boy.

"Well, what's *my* wife had?" Dad asked. "I'm not interested in any Mrs. Gilbert, obstetrically or any other way."

"Of course you're not," the nurse apologized. "Just a moment, and I'll see about Mrs. Gilbreth." And then a few minutes later. "Mrs. Gilbreth seems to have checked out of the hospital."

"Checked out? Why she's only been there six hours. Did she have a boy or a girl?"

"Our records don't show that she had either."

"It's got to be one or the other," Dad insisted. "What else is there?"

"I mean," the nurse explained, "she apparently checked out before the baby arrived."

Dad hung up the receiver. "Better start boiling water," he said to Grandma. "Lillie's on the way home."

"With that new baby?"

"No." Dad was downcast. "Somebody else claimed that baby. Lillie apparently put off having hers for the time being."

Mother arrived at the house about half an hour later. She was carrying a suitcase and had walked all the way. Grandma was furious.

"My goodness, Lillie, you have no business out in the street in your condition. And carrying that heavy suitcase. Give it to me. Now get upstairs to bed where you belong. A girl your age should know better. What did you leave the hospital for?"

"I got tired of waiting and I was lonesome. I decided I'd have this one at home, too. Besides, that nurse—she was a fiend. She hid my pencils and notebook and wouldn't even let me read. I never spent a more miserable day."

Lill was born the next day, in Dad's and Mother's room, where pencils and notebooks and proofs were within easy reach of Mother's bed.

"I had already told everybody it was going to be a boy," Dad said, a little resentfully. "But I know it's not your fault, and I think a girl's just fine. I was getting a little sick of boys, anyway. Well, this one will be named for you."

The older children, meanwhile, were becoming curious about where babies came from. The only conclusion we had reached was that Mother always was sick in bed when the babies arrived. About four months after Lill was born, when Mother went to bed early one night with a cold, we were sure a new brother or sister would be on hand in the morning. As soon as we got up, we descended on Dad's and Mother's room.

"Where's the baby? Where's the baby?" we shouted.

"What's all the commotion?" Dad wanted to know. "What's got into you? She's right over there in her crib." He pointed to four-month-old Lill.

"But we want to see the *latest* model," we said. "Come on, Daddy. You can't fool us. Is it a boy or a girl? What are we going to name this one? Come on, Daddy. Where have you hidden him?"

We began looking under the bed and in a half-opened bureau drawer.

"What in the world are you talking about?" Mother said. "There isn't any new baby. Stop pulling all your father's clothes out of that drawer. For goodness sakes, whatever gave you the idea there was a new baby?"

"Well, you were sick, weren't you?" Anne asked.

"I had a cold, yes."

"And every time you're sick, there's always a baby."

"Why, babies don't come just because you're sick," Mother said. "I thought you knew that."

"Then when do they come?" Ern asked. "They always came before when you were sick. You tell us, Daddy."

We had seldom seen Dad look so uncomfortable. "I've got business in town, kids," he said. "In a hurry. Your Mother will tell you. I'm late now." He turned to Mother. "I'd be glad to explain it to them if I had the time," he said. "You go ahead and tell them, Lillie. It's time they knew. I'm sorry I'm rushed. You understand, don't you?"

"I certainly do," said Mother.

Dad hurried down the front stairs and out the front door. He didn't even stop by the dining room for a cup of coffee.

"I'm glad you children asked that question," Mother began. But she didn't look glad at all. "Come and sit here on the bed. It's time we had a talk. In the first place, about the stork—he doesn't really bring babies at all, like some children think."

"We knew that!"

"You did?" Mother seemed surprised. "Well, that's fine. Er— what else do you know?"

"That you have to be married to have babies, and it takes lots of hot water, and sometimes the doctor does things to you that make you holler."

"But not very loud?" Mother asked anxiously. "Never very loud or very often. Am I right?"

"No, never loud or very often."

"Good. Now first let's talk about flowers and bees and . . ."

When she was through, we knew a good deal about botany and something about apiology, but nothing about how babies came. Mother just couldn't bring herself to explain it.

"I don't know what's the matter with Mother," Anne said afterwards. "It's the first time she's ever kept from answering a question. And Daddy went rushing out of the room like he knew where something was buried."

Later we asked Tom Grieves about it. But the only reply we elicited from him was to: "Stop that nasty kind of talk, you evil-minded things you, or I'll tell your father on you."

Dad assumed Mother had told us. Mother assumed she had made her point in the flowers and bees. And we still wondered where babies came from.

Fred was born in Buttonwoods, Rhode Island, where we spent a summer. A hurricane knocked out communications and we couldn't get a doctor. A next-door neighbor who came over to help became so frightened at the whole thing that she kept shouting to Mother:

"Don't you dare have that baby until the doctor comes."

"I'm trying not to," Mother assured her calmly. "There's no use to get all excited. You mustn't get yourself all worked up. It's not good for you. Sit down here on the side of the bed and try to relax."

"Who's having this baby, anyway?" Dad asked the neighbor. "A big help you are!"

He departed for the kitchen to boil huge vats of water, most of which was never used.

Fred, Number Eight, arrived just as the doctor did.

Dan and Jack were born in Providence, and Bob and Jane in Nantucket. Dan and Jack came into the world in routine enough fashion, but Bob arrived all of a sudden. Tom Grieves had to pedal through Nantucket on a bicycle to find the doctor. Since Tom was in pajamas, having been routed from his bed, most of the island knew about Bob's birth. Once again, it was a case of the baby and the doctor arriving simultaneously.

By that time, all the family names for boys had been exhausted. The names of all the uncles, both grandfathers, and the four great grandfathers had been used. Great uncles were being resurrected from the family Bible and studied carefully.

"Now let's run over the names of the Bunker men again," Dad said, referring to Grandma Gilbreth's brothers. "Samuel? Never could tolerate that name. Nathaniel? Too bookish. Frederick? We got one already. Humphrey? Ugh. Daniel? We got one. Nothing there."

"How about the middle names?" Mother suggested. "Maybe we'll get an idea from the Bunkers' middle names."

"All right. Moses? Too bullrushy. William? We got one. Abraham? They'd call him Abie. Irving? Over my dead body, which would be quite a climb."

"What was your father's name again?" Mother asked.

"John," said Dad. "we got one."

"No, I know that. I mean his middle name."

"You know what it was," said Dad. "We're not having any."

"Oh, that's right," Mother giggled. "Hiram, wasn't it?"

Dad started thumbing impatiently through the Bible. "Jacob? No. Saul? Job, Noah, David? Too sissy. Peter? Paul? John? We got one."

"Robert," Mother said. "That's it. We'll call him Robert."

"Why Robert? Who's named Robert?" Dad looked over the top of his glasses at Mother, and she reddened.

"No one in particular. It's just a beautiful name, that's all. This one will be Robert."

Dad started to tease. "I knew you had a strange collection of beaux during your college days, but which one was Robert? I don't believe I remember your mentioning him. Was he the one whose picture you had with the blazer and mandolin? Or was he the one your sisters told me about who stuttered?"

"Stop it, Frank," said Mother. "You know that's ridiculous."

We took our cue from Dad. "Oh, Mother, Rob-bert is such a beautiful name. Why didn't you name me Rob-bert? May I carry your books home from college, Lillie, dear? Why Rob-bert, you do say the *nicest* things. And so clever, too."

Dad, who knew that Mother's favorite poet was Browning and suspected where the Robert came from, nevertheless bunched the fingers of his right hand, kissed their tips, and threw his hand into the air.

"Ah, Robert," he intoned, "if I could but taste the nectar of thy lips."

"When you're all quite through," Mother said coldly, "I suggest we have a vote on the name I have proposed. And when it comes to discussing old flames, it might be borne in mind that that is a game two can play. I recall . . ."

"We wouldn't think of blighting any school girl romance, would we, kids?" Dad put in hastily. "What do you say we make it 'Robert' unanimously?"

We voted and it was unanimous.

Bob, Number Eleven, made the count six boys and five girls There was considerable partisanship among the family as to the desired sex of the next baby. The boys wanted to remain in the majority; the girls wanted to tie the count at six-all. Dad, of course, wanted another boy. Mother wanted to please Dad, but at the same time thought it would be nice to have a girl for her last child.

Number Twelve was due in June, 1922, and that meant we would be in Nantucket. Mother had vowed she wasn't going to have another baby in our summer house, because the facilities were so primitive. For a time, she debated whether to remain behind at Montclair and have the baby at home there, or whether to go to Nantucket with us and have the baby in a hospital. Finally, with some foreboding because of her previous experience in Providence, she chose the latter alternative. Jane, Number Twelve, was born in the Nantucket Cottage Hospital.

Mother's ten days in the hospital were pure misery for Dad. He fidgeted and sulked, and said he couldn't get any work done without her. Dad's business trips to Europe sometimes kept him away from home for months, but then he was on the go and in a different environment. Now, at home with the family where he was accustomed to have Mother at his side, he felt frustrated, and seized every opportunity to go down to the hospital and visit.

His excuse to us, when we complained we were being neglected, was that he had to get acquainted with his new daughter.

"I won't be gone long," he'd say. "Anne, you're in charge while I'm away." He'd jump into the car and we wouldn't see him again for hours.

He had never taken such care with his dress. His hair was smoothed to perfection, his canvas shoes a chaste white, and he looked sporty in his linen knickers, his belted coat with a boutonniere of Queen Anne's Lace, and his ribbed, knee-length hose.

"Gee, Daddy, you look like a groom," we told him.

"Bride or stable?"

"A bridegroom."

"You don't have to tell me I'm a handsome dude," he grinned. "I've got a mirror, you know. Well, I've got to make a good impression on that new daughter of mine. What did we name her? Jane."

At the hospital, he'd sit next to Mother's bed and discuss the work he'd planned for the autumn.

"Now I want you to stay here until you feel good and strong. Get a good rest; it's the first rest you've had since the children started coming." And then in the same breath. "I'll certainly be glad when you're back home. I can't seem to get any work accomplished when you're not there."

Mother thought the hospital was marvellous. "I would have to wait until my dozenth baby was born to find out how much better it is to have them in a hospital. The nurses here wait on me hand and foot. You don't know what a comfort it is to have your baby in the hospital."

"No," said Dad, "I don't. And I hope to Heaven I never find out!"

What Mother liked best about the hospital, although she didn't tell Dad, was the knowledge that if she made any noise during the delivery, it didn't matter.

When Dad finally drove Mother and Jane home, he lined all of us up by ages on the front porch. Jane, in her bassinet, was at the foot of the line.

"Not a bad-looking crowd if I do say so myself," he boasted, strutting down the line like an officer inspecting his men. "Well, Lillie, there you have them, and it's all over. Have you stopped to think that by this time next year we won't need a bassinet any more? And by this time two years from now, there won't be a diaper in the house, or baby bottles, or play pens, or nipples—when I think of the equipment we've amassed during the years! Have you thought what it's going to be like not to have a baby in our room? For the first time in seventeen years, you'll be able to go to bed without setting the alarm clock for a two o'clock feeding."

"I've been thinking about that," said Mother. "It's certainly going to be a luxury, isn't it?"

Dad put his arm around her waist, and tears came to her eyes.

Later that summer, when company came to call, Dad would whistle assembly and then introduce us.

"This one is Anne," he'd say, and she'd step forward and shake hands. "And Ernestine, Martha. . . ."

"Gracious, Mr. Gilbreth. And all of them are yours?"

"Hold on, now. Wait a minute." He'd disappear into the bedroom and come out holding Jane. "You haven't seen the latest model."

But some of the enthusinasm had gone out of his tone, because he knew the latest model really was the last model, and that he would never again be able to add the clincher, which so embarrassed Mother, about how another baby was underway.

CHAPTER 1 4

Flash Powder and Funerals

NEXT to motion study and astronomy, photography was the science nearest to Dad's heart. He had converted most of the two-story barn in Montclair into a photographic laboratory. It was here that Mr. Coggin, Dad's English photographer, held forth behind a series of triple-locked doors. Children made Mr. Coggin nervous, particularly when they opened the door of his darkroom when he was in the middle of developing a week's supply of film. Even in front of Dad and Mother, he referred to us as blighters and beggars. Behind their backs, he called us 'orse thieves, bloody barsteds, and worse.

At one time,shortly after Dad had had an addition built on our cottage at Nantucket, he told Mr. Coggin:

"I want you to go up there and get some pictures of the ell on the house."

"Haw," said Mr. Coggin. "I've taken many a picture of the 'ell *in*

155

your 'ouse. But this will be the first time I've taken one of the 'ell *on* your 'ouse."

When Mr. Coggin departed after the unfortunate debacle concerning our tonsils, a series of other professional cameramen came and went. Dad always thought, and with some justification, that none of the professionals were as good a photographer as he. Consequently, when it came to taking pictures of the family, Dad liked to do the job himself.

He liked to do the job as often as possible, rain or shine, day or night, summer or winter, and especially on Sundays. Most photographers prefer sunlight for their pictures. But Dad liked it best when there was no sun and he had an excuse to take his pictures indoors. He seemed to have a special affinity for flashlight powder, and the bigger the flash the more he enjoyed it.

He'd pour great, gray mountains of the powder into the pan at the top of his T-shaped flash gun, and hold this as far over his head as possible with his left hand, while he burrowed beneath a black cloth at the stern of the camera. In his right hand, he'd hold the shutter release and a toy of some kind, which he'd shake and rattle to get our attention.

Probably few men have walked away from larger flashlight explosions than those Dad set off as a matter of routine. The ceilings of some of the rooms in Montclair bore charred, black circles, in mute testimony to his intrepidity as an exploder. Some of the professional photographers, seeing him load a flash gun, would blanch, mutter, and hasten from the room.

"I know what I'm doing," Dad would shout after them irritably. "Go ahead, then, if you don't want to learn anything. But when I'm through, just compare the finished product with the kind of work you do."

The older children had been through it so often that, while some-what shellshocked, they were no longer terrified. It would be stretch-ing a point to say they had developed any real confidence in Dad's indoor photography. But at least they had adopted a fatalistic atti-tude that death, if it came, would be swift and painless. The younger children, unfortunately, had no such comforting philosophy to fall back on. Even the Latest Model was aware that all hell was liable to break loose at any time after Dad submerged under the black cloth. They'd behave pretty well right up to the time Dad was going to take the picture. Then they'd start bellowing.

"Lillie, stop those children from crying," Dad would shout from under the black cloth. "Dan, open your eyes and take your fingers out of your ears! The idea! Scared of a little flash! And stop that fidg-eting, all of you."

He'd come up in disgust from under the cloth. It was hot under there, and the bending over had made the blood run to his head.

"Now stop crying, all of you," he'd say furiously. "Do you hear me? Next time I go under there I want to see all of you smiling."

He'd submerge again. "I said stop that crying. Now smile, or I'll come out and give you something to cry about. Smile so I can see the whites of your teeth. That's more like it."

He'd slip a plate holder into the back of the camera.

"Ready? Ready? Smile now. Hold it. Hold it. Hooold it."

He'd wave the toy furiously and then there'd be an awful, blind-ing, roaring flash that shook the room and deposited a fine ash all over us and the floor. Dad would come up, sweaty but grinning. He'd look to see whether the ceiling was still there, and then put down the flash gun and go over and open the windows to let out a cloud of choking smoke that made your eyes water.

"I think that was a good picture," he'd say. "And this new flash gun certainly works fine. Don't go away now. I want to take one more as soon as the smoke clears. I'm not sure I had quite enough light that time."

For photographs taken in the sunlight, Dad had a delayed-action release that allowed him to click the camera and then run and get into the picture himself before the shutter was released. While outdoor pictures did away with the hazard of being blown through the ceiling, they did not eliminate the hazards connected with Dad's temper.

The most heavily relied upon prop for outdoor pictures was the family Pierce Arrow, parked with top down in the driveway.

Once we were seated to Dad's satisfaction, he would focus, tell us to smile, click the delayed-action release, and race for the driver's seat. He'd arrive there panting, and the car would lurch as he jumped in. When conditions were ideal, there would be just enough time for Dad to settle himself and smile pleasantly, before the camera clicked off the exposure.

Conditions were seldom ideal, for the delayed action release was unreliable. Sometimes it went off too soon, thus featuring Dad's blurred but ample stern as he climbed into the car. Sometimes it didn't go off for a matter of minutes, during which we sat tensely, with frozen-faced smiles, while we tried to keep the younger children from squirming. Dad, with the camera side of his mouth twisted into a smile, would issue threats from the other side about what he was going to do to all of us if we so much as twitched a muscle or batted an eyelash.

Occasionally, when the gambling instinct got the better of him, he'd try to turn around and administer one swift disciplinary stroke, and then turn back again in time to smile before the camera went off. Once, when he lost the gamble, an outstanding action picture

resulted, which showed Dad landing a well-aimed and well-deserved clout on the side of Frank's head.

Any number of pictures showed various members of the family, who had received discipline within a matter of seconds before the shutter clicked, looking anything but pleasant in the swivel seats of the car. The swivel seat occupants received most of the discipline, because they were the easiest for Dad to reach, and no one liked to sit there when it was picture taking time.

Sometimes newspaper photographers and men from Underwood and Underwood would come to the house to take publicity pictures. Dad would whistle assembly, take out his stopwatch, and demonstrate how quickly we could gather. Then he would show the visitors how we could type, send the Morse code, multiply numbers, and speak some French, German, and Italian. Sometimes he'd holler *"fire"* and we'd drop to the floor and roll up in rugs.

Everything seemed to go much smoother when Dad was on our side of the camera, for now he too was ordered where to stand, when to lick his lips, and, occasionally, to stop fidgeting. The rest of us had no trouble looking pleasant after the photographer lectured Dad. In fact we looked so pleasant we almost popped.

"Mr. Gilbreth, will you please stand still? And take your hands out of your pockets. Move a little closer to Mrs. Gilbreth. No, not that close. Look. I want you right here." The photographer would take him by the arm and place him. "Now try to look pleasant, please."

"By jingo, I am looking pleasant," Dad finally would say impatiently.

"I can't understand one thing," a man from Underwood and Underwood told Dad one time after the picture-taking was over. "I've been out here several times now. Everything always seems to be going fine until I put my head under the black cloth to focus. Then, just as if it's a signal, the four youngest ones start to cry and I never can get them to stop until I put the cloth out of sight."

"Is that a fact?" was all the information Dad volunteered.

Dad had a knack for setting up publicity pictures that tied in with his motion-study projects. While he was working for the Remington people, there were the news reels of us typing touch system on Moby Dick, the white typewriter with the blind keys. Later, when he got a job with an automatic pencil company, he decided to photograph us burying a pile of wooden pencils.

We were in Nantucket at the time. Tom Grieves built a realistic-looking black coffin out of a packing case. For weeks we bought and collected wooden pencils, until we had enough to fill the coffin.

We carried the casket to a sand dune between *The Shoe* and the ocean, where Dad and Tom dug a shallow grave. It was a desolate, windswept spot. The neighbors on the Cliff, doubtless concluding that one of us had fallen down and had had to be destroyed, watched our actions through binoculars.

Dad set up a still camera on a tripod, connected the delayed-action attachment, and took a series of pictures showing us lowering the coffin into the grave and covering it with sand.

"We'll have to dig up the coffin now and do the same thing all over again so we can get the movies," Dad said. "We're going to hit them coming and going with this one."

We dug, being careful not to scratch up the coffin, and then sifted the sand from the pencils. Tom cranked the movie camera while we went through the second funeral. Fortunately, it was before the days of sound movies, because Dad kept hollering instructions.

"Turn that crank twice a second, Tom. And one and two and

three and four. Get out from in front of the camera, Ernestine. Marguerite Clark and Mary Pickford have things pretty well lined up out there, you know. Now then, everybody pick up the shovels and heave in the sand. Look serious. This is a sad burial. The good are often interred with their bones. So may it be with pencils. And one and two and . . ."

When we were through with the second funeral, Dad told us we'd have to dig up the coffin again.

"You're not going to take any more pictures, are you?" we begged. "We've taken the stills and the movies."

"Of course not," said Dad. "But you don't think we're going to waste all those perfectly good wooden pencils, do you? Dig them up and take them back into the house. They should last us for years."

In justification to Dad, it should be said that automatic pencils always were used once the supply of wooden ones was exhausted. Dad simply couldn't stand seeing the wooden ones wasted.

The next summer, when Dad was hired as a consultant by a washing machine company, we went through the same procedure with the washboard and hand-wringer at Nantucket. This time, though, Tom was prepared.

"Wait a minute, Mr. Gilbreth," he said. "Before you bury my wringer I want to oil it good, so I can get the sand off if when we dig it up again."

"That might not be a bad idea," Dad admitted. "After all," he added defensively, "I bought you a washing machine for Montclair. I can't have washing machines scattered all along the Atlantic seaboard, you know."

"I didn't say nothing," said Tom. "I just said I wanted to oil my wringer good, that's all. I didn't say nothing about a washing machine for Nantucket." He started to mutter. "Efficiency. All I hear around this house is efficiency. I'd like to make one of them lectures about efficiency. The one best way to ruin a wringer is to bury the God-damned thing in the sand, and then dig it up again. That's motion study for you!"

"What's that?" asked Dad. "Speak up if you have anything to say, and if you haven't keep quiet."

Tom continued muttering. "Motion study is burying a God-damned wringer in the sand and getting the parts all gummed up so that it breaks your back to turn it. That's motion study, as long as it's someone else's motions your studying, and not your own. Lincoln freed the slaves. All but one. All but one."

The pictures and writeups sometimes put us on the defensive in school and among our friends.

"How come you write with a wooden pencil in school, when I saw in the newsreel how your father and all you kids buried a whole casket of them in a grave?"

Sometimes, and this was worst of all, the teachers would read excerpts from writeups about the process charts in the bathroom, the language records, and the decisions of the Family Council. We'd blush and squirm, and wish Dad had a nice job selling shoes somewhere, and that he had only one or two children, neither of whom was us.

The most dangerous reporters, from our standpoint, were the women who came to interview Mother for human interest stories. Mother usually got Dad to sit in on such interviews, because she liked to be able to prove to him and us that she didn't say any of the things they attributed to her, or at least not many of them.

Dad derived considerable pleasure from reading these interviews aloud at the supper table, with exaggerated gestures and facial expressions that were supposed to be Mother's.

"There sat Mrs. Gilbreth, surrounded by her brood, reading aloud a fairy tale," Dad would read. "The oldest, almost debutante Anne, wants to be a professional violinist. Ernestine intends to be a painter, Martha and Frank to follow in their father's footsteps."

" 'Tell me about your honorary degrees,' I asked this remarkable mother of twelve. A flush of crimson crept modestly to her cheeks, and she made a depreciating moue."

Here Dad would stop long enough to give his version of a depreciating moue, and hide his face coyly behind an upraised elbow. He resumed reading:

" 'I am far more proud of my dozen husky, red-blooded American children than I am of my two dozen honorary degrees and my membership in the Czechoslovak Academy of Science,' Mrs. Gilbreth told me."

"Mercy, Maud," Mother exploded. "I never said anything like that. You were there during that interview, Frank. Where did that woman get all that? If my mother should see that article, I don't know what she'd think of me. That woman never asked me about honorary degrees. And two dozen? No one ever had two dozen, unless it was poor Mr. Wilson. And I never said a thing about Czechoslovakia. And I hate and detest people who make depreciating moues. I never made one in my life, or at any rate not since I've been old enough to know better."

Meanwhile, both Anne and Ern were near tears.

"I can't go back to school tomorrow," Anne said. "How can I face the class after that business about the violin?"

"How about me?" moaned Ern. "At least you own a violin and

can make noises come out of it. 'Ernestine wants to be a painter.' How *could* you tell her that, Mother? And my teacher is sure to read it out loud. She always does."

"I didn't tell her that or anything else in the article," Mother insisted. "Where do you suppose she dreamed up those things, Frank?"

Dad grinned and went on reading.

"Mr. Gilbreth, the time study expert, entered the room on tiptoe so as not to disturb his wife's train of thought. Plump but dynamic, Mr. Gilbreth . . ."

The grin faded and Dad tossed the newspaper from him in disgust. "What unspeakable claptrap," he grunted. "Of all the words in the English language, the one I like least is 'plump.' The whole article is just a figment of the imagination."

One newsreel photographer, who visited us in Nantucket, deliberately set out to make us look ridiculous. It wasn't a difficult job. If he was acting under instructions from his employers, he should have been paid a bonus.

In good faith, Dad moved the dining room table, the chairs and his pew out onto the beach grass at the side of our cottage, where the newsreel man said the light would be best. There, amid the sandflies, we ate dinner while the cameraman took pictures.

The newsreel, as shown in the movie houses, opened with a caption which said, "The family of Frank B. Gilbreth, time-saver, eats dinner." The rest of it was projected at about ten times the normal speed. It gave the impression that we raced to the table, passed plates madly in all directions, wolfed our food, and ran away from the table, all in about forty-five seconds. In the background was the reason the photographer wanted us outside— the family laundry with, of course, the diapers predominating.

We saw the newsreel at the Dreamland Theater in Nantucket, and it got much louder laughs than the comedy, which featured a fat actor named Lloyd Hamilton. Everyone in the Dreamland turned around and gaped at us, and we were humiliated and furious. We didn't even want to go to Coffin's Drug Store for a soda, when Dad extended a half-hearted invitation after the show.

"I hope it never comes to the Wellmont in Montclair," we kept repeating. "How can we ever go back to school?"

"Well," Dad said, "it was a mean trick, all right, and I'd like to get my hands on that photographer. But it could have been worse. Do you know what I kept thinking all the way through it? I kept thinking that when it was over they probably were going to show it again, backwards, so that it would look as if we were re-gurgitating our food back on our plates. I'll swear, if they had done that I was going to wreck the place."

"And I would have helped you," said Mother. "Honestly!"

"Come on, it's water over the dam," Dad shrugged. "Let's forget it. Let's go up to Coffin's after all and get those sodas. I'm ready for a double chocolate soda. What do you say?"

Under such relentless arm-twisting, we finally gave in and allowed ourselves to be taken to Coffin's.

CHAPTER 15

Gilbreths and Company

DAD'S theories ranged from Esperanto, which he made us study because he thought it was the answer to half the world's problems, to immaculate conception, which he said wasn't supported by available biological evidence. His theories on social poise, although requiring some minor revision as the family grew larger, were constant to the extent that they hinged on unaffectation.

A poised, unaffected person was never ridiculous, at least in his own mind, Dad told us. And a man who didn't feel ridiculous could never lose his dignity. Dad seldom felt ridiculous, and never admitted losing his dignity.

The part of the theory requiring some revision was that guests would feel at home if they were treated like one of our family. As Mother pointed out, and Dad finally admitted, the only guest who could possibly feel like a member of our family was a guest

167

who, himself, came from a family of a dozen, headed by a motion study man.

When guests weren't present, Dad worked at improving our table manners. Whenever a child within his reach took too large a mouthful of food, Dad's knuckles would descend sharply on the top of the offender's head, with a thud that made Mother wince.

"Not on the head, Frank," she protested in shocked tones. "For mercy sakes, not on the head!"

Dad paid no attention except when the blow had been unusually hard. In such cases he rubbed his knuckles ruefully and replied:

"Maybe you're right. There must be softer places."

If the offender was at Mother's end of the table, out of Dad's reach, he'd signal her to administer the skull punishment. Mother, who never disciplined any of us or even threatened discipline, ignored the signals. Dad then would catch the eye of a child sitting near the offender and, by signals, would deputize him to carry out the punishment.

"With my compliments," Dad would say when the child with the full mouth turned furiously on the one who had knuckled him. "If I've told you once, I've told you a hundred times to cut your food up into little pieces. How am I going to drive that into your skull?"

"Not on the head," Mother repeated. "Mercy, Maud, not on the head!"

Anyone with an elbow on the table might suddenly feel his wrist seized, raised and jerked downward so that his elbow hit the table hard enough to make the dishes dance.

"Not on the elbow, Frank. That's the most sensitive part of the body. Any place but on the elbow."

Mother disapproved of all forms of corporal punishment. She felt, though, that she could achieve better results in the long run by objecting to the part of the anatomy selected for the punishment, rather than the punishment itself. Even when Dad administered vitally needed punishment on the conventional area, the area where it is supposed to do the most good, Mother tried to intervene.

"Not on the end of the spine," she'd say in a voice indicating her belief that Dad was running the risk of crippling us for life. "For goodness sakes, not on the end of the spine!"

"Where, then?" Dad shouted furiously in the middle of one spanking. "Not on the top of the head, not on the side of the ear, not on the back of the neck, not on the elbow, not across the legs, and not on the seat of the pants. Where did your father spank you? Across the soles of the by jingoed feet like the heathen Chinese?"

"Well, not on the end of the spine," Mother said. "You can be sure of that."

Skull-rapping and elbow-thumping became a practice in which everybody in the family, except Mother, participated until Dad deemed our table manners satisfactory. Even the youngest child could mete out the punishment without fear of reprisal. All during meals, we watched each other, and particularly Dad, for an opportunity. Sometimes the one who spotted a perched elbow would sneak out of his chair and walk all the way around the table, so that he could catch the offender.

Dad was quite careful about his elbows, but every so often would forget. It was considered a feather in one's cap to thump any elbow. But the ultimate achievement was to thump Dad's. This was considered not just a feather in the cap, but the entire head-dress of a full Indian chief.

When Dad was caught and his elbow thumped, he made a great to-do over it. He grimaced as if in excruciating pain, sucked in air through his teeth, rubbed the elbow, and claimed he couldn't use his arm for the remainder of the meal.

Occasionally, he would rest an elbow purposely on the edge of the table, and make believe he didn't notice some child who had slipped out of a chair and was tiptoeing toward him. Just as the child was about to reach out and grab the elbow, Dad would slide it into his lap.

"I've got eyes in the back of my head," Dad would announce.

The would-be thumper, walking disappointedly back to his chair, wondered if it wasn't just possible that Dad really did.

Both Dad and Mother tried to impress us that it was our responsibility to make guests feel at home. There were guests for meals almost as often as not, particularly business friends of Dad's, since his office was in the house. There was no formality and no special preparations except a clean napkin and an extra place at the table.

"If a guest is sitting next to you, it's your job to keep him happy, to see that things are passed to him," Dad kept telling us.

George Isles, a Canadian author, seemed to Lillian to be an unhappy guest. Mr. Isles was old, and told sad but fascinating stories.

"Once upon a time there was an ancient, poor man whose joints hurt when he moved them, whose doctor wouldn't let him smoke cigars, and who had no little children to love him," Mr. Isles said. He continued with what seemed to us to be a tale of overwhelming loneliness, and then concluded:

"And do you know who that old man was?"

We had an idea who it was, but we shook our heads and said we didn't. Mr. Isles looked sadder than ever. He slowly raised his forearm and tapped his chest with his forefinger.

"Me," he said.

Lillian, who was six, was sitting next to Mr. Isles. It was her responsibility to see that he was happy, and she felt somehow that she had failed on the job. She threw her arms around his neck and kissed his dry, old man's cheek.

"You do too have little children who love you," she said, on the brink of tears. "You do too!"

Whenever Mr. Isles came to call after that, he always brought one box of candy for Mother and us, and a separate box for Lillian. Ernestine used to remark, in a tone tinged with envy, that Lill was probably New Jersey's youngest gold digger, and that few adult gold diggers ever had received more, in return for less.

Dad was an easy-going host, informal and gracious, and we tried to pattern ourselves after him.

"Any more vegetables, boss?" he'd ask Mother. "No? Well, how about mashed potatoes? Lots of them. And plenty of lamb. Fine. Well, Sir, I can't offer you any vegetables, but how about . . . ?"

"Oh, come on, have some more beef," Frank urged a visiting German engineer. "After all, you've only had three helpings."

"There's no need to gobble your grapefruit like a pig," Fred told a woman professor from Columbia University, who had arrived late and was trying to catch up with the rest of us. "If we finish ahead of you, we'll wait until you're through."

"I'm sorry, but I'm afraid I can't pass your dessert until you finish your lima beans," Dan told a guest on another occasion.

"Daddy won't allow it, and you're my responsibility. Daddy says a Belgian family could live a week on what's thrown away in this house every day."

"Daddy, do you think that what Mr. Fremonville is saying is of general interest?" Lill interrupted a long discourse to ask.

Dad and Mother, and most of the guests, laughed away remarks like these without too much embarrassment. Dad would apologize and explain the family rule involved, and the reason for it. After the guests had gone, Mother would get us together and tell us that while family rules were important, it was even more important to see that guests weren't made uncomfortable.

Sometimes after a meal, Dad's stomach would rumble and, when there weren't any guests, we'd tease him about it. The next time it rumbled, he'd look shocked and single out one of us.

"Billy," he said. "Please! I'm not in the mood for an organ recital."

"That was your stomach, not mine, Daddy. You can't fool me."

"You children have the noisiest stomachs I've ever heard. Don't you think so, Lillie?"

Mother looked disapprovingly over her mending.

"I think," she said, "there are Eskimos in the house."

One night, Mr. Russell Allen, a young engineer, was a guest for supper. Jack, in a high chair across the table from him, accidentally swallowed some air and let out a belch that resounded through the dining room and, as we found out later, was heard even in the kitchen by Mrs. Cunningham. It was such a thorough burp, and had emerged from such a small subject, that all conversation was momentarily suspended in amazement. Jack, more surprised than anybody, looked shocked. He reached out his arm and pointed a chubby and accusing forefinger at the guest.

"Mr. Allen," he said in offended dignity. "Please! I'm not in the mood for an organ recital."

"Why, Jackie!" said Mother, almost in tears."Why, Jackie. How could you?"

"Out," roared Dad. "Skiddoo. Tell Mrs. Cunningham to give you the rest of your supper in the kitchen. And I'll see you about this later."

"Well, you say it," Jack sobbed as he disappeared toward the kitchen. "You say it when your stomach rumbles."

Dad was blushing. The poise which he told us he valued so highly had disappeared. He shifted uneasily in his seat and fumbled with his napkin. Nobody could think of a way to break the uneasy silence.

Dad cleared his throat with efficient thoroughness. But the silence persisted, and it hung heavily over the table.

"Lackaday," Dad finally said. The situation was getting desperate, and he tried again. "Lack a couple of days," Dad said with a weak, artificial laugh. We felt sorry for him and for Mother and Mr. Allen, who were just as crimson as Dad. The silence persisted.

Dad suddenly flung his napkin on the table and walked out into the kitchen. He returned holding Jack by the hand. Jack was still crying.

"All right, Jackie," Dad said. "Come back and sit down. You're right, you learned it from me. First you apologize to Mr. Allen. Then we'll tell him the whole story. And then none of us will ever say it again. As your Mother told us, it all comes from having Eskimos in the house."

Dad's sister, Aunt Anne, was an ample Victorian who wore full, sweeping skirts and high ground-gripper shoes. She was older than Dad, and they were much alike and devoted to each other. She was kindly but stern, big bosomed, and every inch a lady. Like Dad, she had reddish brown hair and a reddish brown temper. She, her husband, and their grown children, whom we worshipped, lived a few blocks from us in Providence. Aunt Anne was an accomplished pianist and gave music lessons at her house at 26 Cabot Street. Dad thought it would be nice if all of us learned to play something. Dad admitted he was as green as any valley when it came to music, but he had a good ear and he liked symphonies.

Aunt Anne must have sensed almost immediately that we had no talent. She knew, though, that any such admission would have a depressing effect on Dad, who took it for granted that his children had talent for everything. Consequently, Aunt Anne stuck courageously to a losing cause for six years, in an unusual display of devotion and fortitude above and beyond the regular call of family duty.

When she finally became convinced of the hopelessness of teaching us the piano, she shifted us to other instruments. Although we had no better success, the other instruments at least were quieter than the piano and, more important, only one person could play them at a time.

Our Anne was shifted to the violin, Ernestine to the mandolin, and Martha and Frank to the 'cello. It was awful at home when we practiced, and Dad would walk smirking through the house with wads of cotton sticking prominently from his ears.

"Never mind," he said, when we told him we didn't seem to

be making any progress. "You stick with it. You'll thank me when you're my age."

Unselfishly jeopardizing her professional reputation as a teacher, Aunt Anne always allowed each of us to play in the annual recitals at her music school. Usually we broke down in the middle, and always had a demoralizing effect on the more talented children, and on their parents in the audience.

To salvage what she could of her standing as a teacher, Aunt Anne used to tell the audience before we went on stage that we had only recently shifted from the piano to stringed instruments. The implication, although not expressed in so many words, was that we had already mastered the piano and were now branching out along other musical avenues.

Just before we started to play, she affixed mutes to our strings and whispered:

"Remember, your number should be played softly, softly as a little brook tinkling through a still forest."

The way we played, it didn't tinkle. As Dad whispered to Mother at one recital: "If I heard that coming from the back fence at night, I'd either report it to the police or heave shoes at it."

Aunt Anne was good to us and we loved her and her family, but like Dad she insisted on having her own way. While we reluctantly accepted Dad's bossing as one of the privileges of his rank as head of the family, we had no intention of accepting it from anybody else, including his oldest sister.

After we moved to Montclair, Aunt Anne came to stay with us for several days while Mother and Dad were away on a lecture tour. She made it plain from the start that she was not a guest, but the temporary commander-in-chief. She even used the front stairs, leading from the front hall to the second floor, instead of the back stairs, which led from the kitchen to a hallway near the girls' bathroom. None of us was allowed to use the front stairs, because Dad wanted to keep the varnish on them looking nice.

"Daddy will be furious if he comes home and finds you've been using his front stairs," we told Aunt Anne.

"Nonsense," she cut us off. "The back stairs are narrow and steep, and I for one don't propose to use them. As long as I'm here, I'll use any stairs I have a mind to. Now rest your features and mind your business."

She sat at Dad's place at the foot of the table, and we resented this, too. Ordinarily, Frank, as the oldest boy, sat in Dad's place, and Anne, as the oldest girl, sat at Mother's. We also disapproved of Aunt Anne's blunt criticism of how we kept our bedrooms, and some of the changes she made in the family routine.

"What do you do, keep pigeons in here?" she'd say when she walked into the bedroom shared by Frank an Bill. "I'm coming back in fifteen minutes, and I want to find this room in apple-pie order."

And: "I don't care what time your regular bedtime is. As long as I'm in charge, we'll do things my way. Off with you now."

Like Grandma and Dad, Aunt Anne thought that all Irishmen were shiftless and that Tom Grieves was the most shiftless of all Irishmen. She told him so at least once a day, and Tom was scared to death of her.

Experience has established the fact that a person cannot move from a small, peaceful home into a family of a dozen without having something finally snap. We saw this happen time after time with Dad's stenographers and with the cooks who followed Mrs. Cunningham. In order to reside with a family of a dozen it is necessary either (1) to be brought up from birth in such a family, as we were; or (2) to become acustomed to it as it grew, as Dad, Mother, and Tom Grieves did.

It was at the dinner table that something finally snapped in Aunt Anne.

We had spent the entire meal purposely making things miserable for her. Bill had hidden under the table, and we had removed his place and chair so she wouldn't realize he was missing. While we ate, Billy thumped Aunt Anne's legs with the side of his hand.

"Who's kicking me?" she complained. "Saints alive!"

We said no one.

"Well, you don't have a dog, do you?"

We didn't, and we told her so. Our collie had died some time before this.

"Well somebody's certainly kicking me. Hard."

She insisted that the child sitting on each side of her slide his chair toward the head of the table, so that no legs could possibly reach her. Bill thumped again.

"Somebody *is* kicking me," Aunt Anne said, "and I intend to get to the bottom of it. Literally."

Bill thumped again. Aunt Anne picked up the table cloth and looked under the table, but Bill had anticipated her and retreated to the other end. The table was so long you couldn't see that far underneath without getting down on your hands and knees, and Aunt Anne was much too dignified to stoop to any such level. When she put the table cloth down again, Bill crawled forward and licked her hand.

"You do too have a dog," Aunt Anne said accusingly, while she dried her hand on a napkin. "Speak up now! Who brought that miserable cur into the house?"

Bill thumped her again and retreated. She picked up the table cloth and looked. She put it down again, and he licked her hand. She looked again, and then dangled her hand temptingly between her knees. Bill couldn't resist this trap, and this time Aunt Anne was ready for him. When he started to lick, she snapped her knees together like a vice, trapped his head in the folds of her skirt, and reached down and grabbed him by the hair.

"Come out of there, you scamp you," she shouted. "I've got you. You can't get away this time. Come out, I say."

She didn't give Bill a chance to come out under his own power. She yanked, and he came out by the hair of his head, screaming and kicking.

In those days, Bill was not a snappy dresser. He liked old clothes, preferably held together with safety pins, and held up by old neckties. When he wore a necktie around his neck, which was as seldom as possible, he sometimes evened up the ends by trimming the longer with a pair of scissors. His knickers usually were partially unbuttoned in the front—what the Navy calls the commodore's privilege. They were completely unfastened at the legs and hung down to his ankles. During the course of a day, his stockings rode gradually down his legs and, by dinner, had partially disappeared into his sneakers. When Mother was at home, she made him wear such appurtanences as a coat and a belt. In her absence, he had grown slack.

When Aunt Anne jerked him out, a piece of string connecting a buttonhole in his shirt with a buttonhole in the front of his trousers suddenly broke. Bill grabbed for his pants, but it was too late.

Vasiliu

"Go to your room, you scamp you," Aunt Anne said, shaking him. "Just wait until your father comes home. He'll know how to take care of you."

Bill picked up his knickers and did as he was told. He had a new respect for Aunt Anne, and the whole top of his head was smarting from the hair-pulling.

Aunt Anne sat down with deceptive calm, and gave us a disarming smile.

"I want you children to listen carefully to me," she almost whispered. "There's not a living soul here, including the baby, who is cooperative. I've never seen a more spoiled crowd of children."

As she went on, her voice grew louder. Much louder. Tom Grieves opened the pantry door a crack and peeked in.

"For those of you who like to believe that an only child is a selfish child, let me say you are one hundred per cent wrong. From what I have seen, this is the most completely selfish household in the entire world."

She was roaring now, wide open, and it was the first time we had ever seen her that way. Except that her voice was an octave higher, it might have been Dad, sitting there in his own chair.

"From this minute on, pipe down every last one of you, or I'll lambaste the hides off you. I'll fix you so you can't sit down for a month. Do you understand? Does everybody understand? In case you don't realize it, *I've had enough!*"

With that, determined to show us she wasn't going to let us spoil her meal, she put a piece of pie in her mouth. But she was so upset that she choked, and slowly turned a deep purple. She clutched at her throat. We were afraid she was dying, and were ashamed of ourselves.

Tom, watching at the door, saw his duty. Putting aside his fear of her, he ran into the dining room and slapped her on the back. Then he grabbed her arms and held them high over her head.

"You'll be all right in a minute, Aunt Anne," he said.

His system worked. She gurgled and finally caught her breath. Then, remembering her dignity, she jerked her arms out of his hands and drew herself up to her full height.

"Keep your hands to yourself, Grieves," she said in a tone that indicated her belief that his next step would be to loosen her corset."Don't ever let me hear you make the fatal mistake of calling me 'Aunt Anne' again. And after this, mind your own"— she looked slowly around the table and then decided to say it anyway—"*damned* business."

There was no doubt after that about who was boss, and Aunt Anne had no further trouble with us. When Dad and Mother returned home, all of us expected to be disciplined. But we had misjudged Aunt Anne.

"You look like you've lost weight," Dad said to her. "The children didn't give you any trouble, did they?"

"Not a bit," said Aunt Anne. "They behaved beautifully, once we got to understand each other. We got along just fine, didn't we, children?"

She reached out fondly and rumpled Billy's hair, which didn't need rumpling.

"Ouch," Billy whispered to her, grinning in relief. "It still hurts. Have a heart."

We had better success with another guest whom we set out deliberately to discourage. She was a woman psychologist who came to Montclair every fortnight from New York to give us intelligence

tests. It was her own idea, not Dad's or Mother's, but they wel-
comed her. She was planning to publish a paper about the effects
of Dad's teaching methods on our intelligence quotients.

She was thin and sallow, with angular features and a black
moustache, not quite droopy enough to hide a horsey set of upper
teeth. We hated her and suspected that the feeling was mutual.

At first her questions were legitimate enough: Arithmetic, spelling, languages, geography, and the sort of purposeful confusion—
about ringing numbers and underlining words—in which some
psychologists place particular store.

After we had completed the initial series of tests, she took us
one by one into the parlor for personal interviews. Even Mother
and Dad weren't allowed to be present.

The interviews were embarrassing and insulting.

"Does it hurt when your mother spanks you?" she asked each
of us, peering searchingly into our eyes and breathing into our
faces. "You mean your mother never spanks you?" She seemed
disappointed. "Well, how about your father? Oh, he does?" That
appeared to be heartening news. "Does your mother pay more
attention to the other children than she does to you? How many
baths do you take a week? Are you sure? Do you think it would be
nice to have still another baby brother? You do? Goodness!"

We decided that if Dad and Mother knew the kinds of questions
we were being asked, they wouldn't like them any better than
we did. Anne and Ernestine had made up their minds to explain
the situation to them, when destiny delivered the psychologist
into our hands, lock, stock and moustache.

Mother had been devising a series of job aptitude tests, and
the desk by her bed was piled with pamphlets and magazines on
psychology. Ernestine was running idly through them one night,

while Mother was reading aloud to us from *The Five Little Peppers and How they Grew*, when she came across a batch of intelligence tests. One of them was the test which the New York woman was in the process of giving us—not the embarrassing personal questions, but the business of circling numbers, spelling, and filling in blanks. The correct answers were in the back.

"Snake's hips," Ernestine crowed. "Got it!"

Mother looked up absently from her book. "Don't mix up my work, Ernie," she said. "What are you after?"

"Just want to borrow something," Ern told her.

"Well, don't forget to put it back when you're through with it, will you? Where was I ? Oh, I remember. Joel had just said that if necessary he could help support the family by selling papers and shining shoes down at the depot."

She resumed her reading.

The psychologist had already given us the first third of the test. Now Anne and Ernestine tutored us on the second third, until we could run right down a page and fill in the answers without even reading the questions. The last third was an oral word-association test, and they coached us on that, too.

"We're going to be the smartest people she ever gave a test to," Ern told us. "And the queerest, too. Make her think we're smart, but uncivilized because we haven't had enough individual attention. That's what she wants to think, anyway."

"Act nervous and queer," Anne said. "While she's talking to you, fidget and scratch yourself. Be as nasty as you can. That won't require much effort from most of you; there's no need our tutoring you on that."

The next time the psychologist came out from New York, she sat us at intervals around the walls of the parlor, with books on our laps to write on. She passed each of us a copy of the second third of the test.

"When I say commence, work as quickly as you can," she told us. "You have half an hour, and I want you to get as far along in the tests as you can. If any of you should happen to finish before the time is up, bring your papers to me." She looked at her watch. "Ready? Now turn your test papers over and start. Remember, I'm watching you, so don't try to look at your neighbor's paper."

We ran down the pages, filling in the blanks. The older children turned in their papers within ten minutes. Lillian, the youngest being examined, finally turned hers in within twenty.

The psychologist looked at Lillian's paper, and her mouth dropped open.

"How old are you, dearie?" she asked.

"Six," said Lill. "I'll be seven in June."

"There's something radically wrong here," the visitor said. "I haven't had a chance to grade all of your paper, but do you know you have a higher I.Q. than Nicholas Murray Butler?"

"I read a lot," Lill said.

The psychologist glanced at the other tests and shook her head.

"I don't know what to think," she sighed. "You've certainly shown remarkable improvement in the last two weeks. Maybe we'd better get on to the last third of the test. I'm going to go around the room and say a word to each of you. I want you to answer instantly the first word that comes into your mind. Now won't that be a nice little game?"

Anne twitched. Ernestine scratched. Martha bit her nails.

"We'll go by ages," the visitor continued. "Anne first."

She pointed to Anne. "Knife," said the psychologist.

"Stab, wound, bleed, slit-throat, murder, disembowel, scream, shriek," replied Anne, without taking a breath and so fast that the words flowed together.

"Jesus," said the psychologist. "Let me get that down. You're just supposed to answer one word, but let me get it all down anyway." She panted in excitement as she scribbled in her pad.

"All right, Ernestine. Your turn. Just one word. 'Black.'"

"Jack," said Ernestine.

The visitor looked at Martha. "Foot."

"Kick," said Martha.

"Hair."

"Louse," said Frank.

"Flower."

"Stink," said Bill.

The psychologist was becoming more and more excited. She looked at Lill.

"Droppings," said Lill, upsetting the apple cart.

"But I haven't even asked you your word yet," the visitor exclaimed. "So that's it. Let me see what your word was going to be. I thought so. Your word was 'bird.' And they told you to say 'droppings,' didn't they?"

Lill nodded sheepishly.

"And they told you just how to fill out the rest of the test, didn't they? I suppose the answers were given to you by your Mother, so you would impress me with how smart you are."

We started to snicker and then to roar. But the psychologist didn't think it was funny.

"You're all nasty little cheats," she said. "Don't think for a minute you pulled the wool over my eyes. I saw through you from the start"

She picked up her wraps and started for the front door. Dad had heard us laughing, and came out of his office to see what was going on. If there was any excitement, he wanted to be in on it.

"Well," he beamed, "it sounds as if it's been a jolly test. Running along so soon? Tell me, frankly, what do you think of my family?"

She looked at us and there was an evil glint in her eye.

"I'm glad you asked me that," she whinnied. "Unquestionably, they are smart. Too damned smart for their breeches. Does that answer your question? As to whether they were aided and abetted in an attempted fraud, I cannot say. But my professional advice is to bear down on them. A good thrashing right now, from the oldest to the youngest, might be just the thing"

She slammed the front door, and Dad looked glumly at us.

"All right," he sighed. "What have you been up to? That woman's going to write a paper on the family. What did you do to her?"

Anne twitched. Ernestine scratched. Martha bit her nails. Dad was getting angry.

"Hold still and speak up. No nonsense!"

"Do you want another baby brother?" Anne asked.

"Does it hurt when your Mother spanks you?" said Ernestine.

"When did you have your last bath?" Martha inquired. "Are you sure? Hmmm?"

Dad raised his hands in surrender and shook his head. He looked old and tired now.

"Sometimes I don't know if it's worth it," he said. "Why didn't you come and tell your Mother and me about it, if she was asking questions like that. Oh, well . . . On the other hand . . . Why the bearded old goat!"

Dad started to smile.

"If she writes a paper about any of that I'll sue her for everything she owns, including her birth certificate. If she has one."

He opened the door into his office.

"Come in and give me all the frightful details."

"After you, Dr. Butler," Ernestine told Lill.

A few minutes later, Mother came into the office, where we were perched on the edges of her and Dad's desks. The stenographers had abandoned their typewriters and were crowded around us.

"What's the commotion, Frank?" she asked Dad. "I could hear you bellowing all the way up in the attic."

"Oh, Lord," Dad wheezed. "Start at the beginning, kids. I want your mother to hear this, too. The bearded old goat—not you, Lillie."

CHAPTER 16

Over the Hill

ON Friday nights, Dad and Mother often went to a lecture or a movie by themselves, holding hands as they went out to the barn to get Foolish Carriage.

But on Saturday nights, Mother stayed home with the babies, while Dad took the rest of us to the movies. We had early supper so that we could get to the theater by seven o'clock, in time for the first show.

"We're just going to stay through one show tonight," Dad told us on the way down. "None of this business about seeing the show through a second time. None of this eleven o'clock stuff. No use to beg me."

When the movie began, Dad became as absorbed as we, and noisier. He forgot all about us, and paid no attention when we nudged him and asked for nickels to put in the candy vendors on the back of the seats. He laughed so hard at the comedies that sometimes he embarrassed us and we tried to tell him that people were looking at him. When the feature was sad, he kept trumpeting his nose and wiping his eyes.

When the lights went on at the end of the first show, we always begged him to change his mind, and let us stay and see it again. He put on an act of stubborn resistance, but always yielded in the end.

"Well, you were less insolent than usual this week," he said. "But I hate to have you stay up until all hours of the night."

"Tomorrow's Sunday. We can sleep late."

"And your mother will give me Hail Columbia when I bring you home late."

"If you think it's all right, Mother will think it's all right."

"Well, all right. We'll make an exception this time. Since your hearts are so set on it, I guess I can sit through it again."

Once, after a whispered message by Ernestine had passed along the line, we picked up our coats at the end of the first show and started to file out of the aisle.

"What are you up to?" Dad called after us in a hurt tone, and loud enough so that people stood up to see what was causing the disturbance. "Where do you think you're going? Do you want to walk home? Come back here and sit down."

We said he had told us on the way to the theater that we could just sit through one show that night.

"Well, don't you want to see it again? After all, you've been good as gold this week. If your hearts are set on it, I guess I could sit through it again. I don't mind, particularly."

We said we were a little sleepy, that we didn't want to be all tired out tomorrow and that we didn't want Mother to be worried because we had stayed out late.

"Aw, come on," Dad begged. "Don't be spoil sports. I'll take care of your mother. Let's see it again. The evening's young. Tomorrow's Sunday. You can sleep late."

We filed smirking back to our seats.

"You little fiends," Dad whispered as we sat down. "You spend hours figuring out ways to gang up on me, don't you? I've got a good mind to leave you all home next week and come to the show by myself."

The picture that made the biggest impression on Dad was a twelve-reel epic entitled *Over the Hill to the Poor House*, or something like that. It was about a wispy widow lady who worked her poor old fingers to the bone for her children, only to end her days in the alms house after they turned against her.

For an hour and a half, while Dad manned the pumps with his handkerchief, the woman struggled to keep her family together. She washed huge vats of clothes. She ironed an endless procession of underwear. Time after time, single-handed and on her hands and knees, she emptied all the cuspidors and scrubbed down the lobby of Grand Central Station.

Her children were ashamed of her and complained because they didn't have store-bought clothes. When the children were grown up, they fought over having her come to live with them. Finally, when she was too old to help even with the housework, they turned her out into the street. There was a snowstorm going on, too.

The fade-out scene, the one that had Dad actually wringing out his handkerchief, showed the old woman, shivering in a worn and inadequate hug-me-tight, limping slowly up the hill to the poor house.

Dad was still red-eyed and blowing his nose while we were drinking our sodas after the movie, and all of us felt depressed.

"I want all of you to promise me one thing," he choked. "No matter what happens to me, I want you to take care of your mother."

After we promised, Dad felt better. But the movie remained on his mind for months.

"I can see myself twenty years from now," he'd grumble when we asked him for advances on our allowances. "I can see myself, old, penniless, unwanted, trudging up that hill. I wonder what kind of food they have at the poor house and whether they let you sleep late in the mornings?"

Even more than the movies, Dad liked the shows that we staged once or twice a year in the parlor, for his and Mother's benefit. The skits, written originally by Anne and Ernestine, never varied much, so we could give them without rehearsal. The skits that Dad liked best were the imitations of him and Mother.

Frank, with a couple of sofa pillows under his belt and a straw hat on the back of his head, played the part of Dad leading us through a factory for which he was a consultant. Ernestine, with stuffed bosom and flowered hat, played Mother. Anne took the part of a superintendent at the factory and the younger children played themselves.

"Is everybody here?" Frank asked Ernestine. She took out a notebook and called the roll. "Is everybody dry? Do you all have your note books? All right, then. Follow me."

We paraded around the room a couple of times in lockstep, like a chain gang, with Frank first, Ernestine next, and the children following by ages. Then we pretended to walk up a flight of stairs, to indicate that we had entered the factory. Anne, the superintendent, came forward and shook hands with Dad.

"Christmas," she said. "Look what followed you in. Are those your children, or is it a picnic?"

"They're my children," Ernestine said indignantly. "And it was no picnic."

"How do you like my little Mongolians?" Frank leered. "Mongolians come cheaper by the dozen, you know. Do you think I should keep them all?"

"I think you should keep them all home," Anne said. "Tell them to stop climbing over my machinery."

"They won't get hurt," Frank assured her. "They're all trained engineers. I trained them myself."

Anne shrieked. "Look at that little Mongolian squatting over my buzz saw." She covered her eyes. "I can't watch him. Don't let him squat any lower. Tell him to stop squatting."

"The little rascal thinks its a bicycle," Frank said. "Leave him alone. Children have to learn by doing."

Someone off stage gave a dying scream.

"I lose more children in factories," Ernestine complained. "Now the rest of you keep away from that buzz saw, you hear me?"

"Someone make a note of that so we can tell how many places to set for supper," Frank said. He turned to Fred. "Freddy boy, I want you to take your fingers out of your mouth, and then explain to the superintendent what's inefficient about this drill press here."

"That thing a drill press?" Fred said with an exaggerated lisp. "Haw."

"Precisely," said Frank. "Explain it to him, in simple language."

"The position of the hand lever is such that there is waste

motion both after transport loaded and transport empty," Fred lisped. "The work plane of the operator is at a fatiguing level and . . ."

Sometimes we made believe we were on an auditorium platform at an engineering meeting, at which Dad was to speak. Anne played the chairman who was introducing him.

"Our next speaker," she said, "is Frank Bunker Gilbreth. Wait a minute now. Please keep your seats. Don't be frightened. He's promised, this time, to limit himself to two hours, and not to mention the 'One Best Way to Do Work' more than twice in the same sentence."

Frank, with pillows in front again, walked to the edge of the platform, adjusted a pince-nez which hung from a black ribbon around his neck, smirked, reached under his coat, and pulled out a manuscript seven inches thick.

"For the purpose of convenience," he began pompously, "I have divided my talk tonight into thirty main headings and one hundred and seventeen sub-headings. I will commence with the first main heading. . . ."

At this point, the other children, who were seated as if they were the engineers in Dad's audience, nudged each other, arose, and tiptoed out of the room. Frank droned on, speaking to an empty hall.

When Frank finally sat down, the audience returned, and the chairman introduced Mother, played again by Ernestine.

"Our next guest is Dr. Lillian Moller Gilbreth. She's not going to make a speech, but she will be glad to answer any questions."

Ernestine swept forward in a wide-brimmed hat and floor-length skirt. She was carrying a suitcase-sized pocketbook, from which protruded a pair of knitting needles, some mending, crochet hook, baby's bottle, and a copy of the *Scientific American.*

She smiled for a full minute, nodding to friends in the audience. "Hello, Grace, I like your new hat. Why, Jennie, you've bobbed your hair. Hello, Charlotte, so glad you could be here."

Dressed in a collection of Mother's best hats, Martha, Frank, Bill and Lill started jumping up with questions.

"Tell us, Mrs. Gilbreth, did you really want such a large family, and if so why?"

"Any other questions?" asked Ernestine.

"Who really wears the pants in your household, Mrs. Gilbreth? You or your husband?"

"Any other questions?" asked Ernestine.

"One thing more, Mrs. Gilbreth. Do Bolivians really come cheaper by the dozen?"

After the skits, Dad sometimes would put on a one-man minstrel show for us, in which he played the parts of both the Messrs. Jones and Bones. We knew the routine by heart, but we always enjoyed it, and so did Dad.

With his lower lip protruding and his hands hanging down to his knees, he shuffled up and down the parlor floor.

"Does you know how you gets de water in de watermelon?"

"I don't know, how does you get the water in the watermelon?"

"Why you plants dem in de spring." Dad slapped his knee, folded his arms in front of his face, and rolled his head to the left and right in spasms of mirth. "Yak. Yak."

"And does you know Isabelle?"

"Isabelle?"

"Yeah, Isabelle necessary on a bicycle."

"And does you know the difference between a pretty girl and

an apple? Well, one you squeeze to git cider, and the odder you git 'sider to squeeze. Yak. Yak."

When the show was over, Dad looked at his watch.

"It's way past your bedtime," he complained. "Doesn't anybody pay any attention to the rules I make? You older children should have been in bed an hour ago, and you little fellows three hours ago."

He took Mother by the arm.

"My throat is as hoarse as a frog's from all that reciting," he said. "The only thing that will soothe it is a nice, sweet, cool, chocolate ice cream soda. With whipped cream. Ummm. He rubbed his stomach. Go to bed, children. Come on, Boss. I'll go get the car and you and I will go down to the drug store. I couldn't sleep a wink with this hoarse throat."

"Take us, Daddy?" we shouted. "You wouldn't go without us? Our throats are hoarse as frogs' too. We wouldn't sleep a wink either."

"See?" Dad asked. "When it comes to sodas, you're right on the job, up and ready to go. But when it comes to going to bed, you're slow as molasses!"

He turned to Mother. "What do you say, Boss?"

Mother protruded her lower lip, sagged her shoulders and let her hands hang down to her knees.

"Did you say mo' 'lasses, Mr. Bones?" she squeaked in a querulous falsetto. "Mo' 'lasses? Why, Honey, I ain't had no 'lasses. Git yo' coats on, chillen. Yak. Yak."

"Thirteen sodas at fifteen cents apiece," Dad muttered. "I can see the handwriting on the wall. Over the Hill to the Poor House."

CHAPTER 17

Four Wheels, No Brakes

BY the time Anne was a senior in high school, Dad was convinced that the current generation of girls was riding, with rouged lips and rolled stockings, straight for a jazzy and probably illicit rendezvous with the greasy-haired devil.

Flaming youth had just caught fire. It was the day of the flapper and the sheik, of petting and necking, of flat chests and dimpled knees. It was yellow slickers with writing on the back, college pennants, and plus fours. Girls were beginning to bob their hair and boys to lubricate theirs. The college boy was a national hero, and collegiate was the most complimentary adjective in the American vocabulary. The ukulele was a social asset second only to the traps and saxophone. It was "Me and the Boy Friend," "Clap Hands Here Comes Charlie" and "Jadda, Jadda, Jing, Jing, Jing." The accepted mode of transportation was the stripped-down

Model T Ford, preferably inscribed with such witticisms as "Chicken, Here's Your Roost," "Four Wheels, No Brakes" and "The Mayflower—Many a Little Puritan Has Come Across In It."

It was the era of unfastened galoshes and the shifters club. It was the start of the Jazz Age.

If people the world over wanted to go crazy, that was their affair, however lamentable. But Dad had no intention of letting his daughters go with them. At least, not without a fight.

"What's the matter with girls today?" Dad kept asking. "Don't they know what those greasy-haired boys are after? Don't they know what's going to happen to them if they go around showing their legs through silk stockings, and with bare knees, and with skirts so short that the slightest wind doesn't leave anything to the imagination?"

"Well, that's the way everybody dresses today," Anne insisted. "Everybody but Ernestine and me; we're school freaks. Boys don't notice things like that when everybody dresses that way."

"Don't try to tell me about boys," Dad said in disgust. "I know all about what boys notice and what they're after. I can see right through all this collegiate stuff. This petting and necking and jazzing are just other words for something that's been going on for a long, long time, only nice people didn't used to discuss it or indulge in it. I hate to tell you what would have happened in my day if girls had come to school dressed like some girls dress today."

"What?" Anne asked eagerly.

"Never you mind. All I know is that even self-respecting street-walkers wouldn't have dressed . . ."

"Frank!" Mother interrupted him. "I don't like that Eskimo word."

The girls turned to Mother for support, but she agreed with Dad.

"After all, men don't want to marry girls who wear makeup and high heels," Mother said. "That's the kind they run around with before they're married. But when it comes to picking out a wife, they want someone they can respect."

"They certainly respect me," Anne moaned. "I'm the most respected girl in the whole high school. The boys respect me so much they hardly look at me. I wish they'd respect me a little less and go out with me a little more. How can you expect me to be popular?"

"Popular!" Dad roared. "Popular. That's all I hear. That's the magic word, isn't it? That's what's the matter with this generation. Nobody thinks about being smart, or clever, or sweet or even attractive. No, sir. They want to be skinny and flat-chested and popular. They'd sell their soul and body to be popular, and if you ask me a lot of them do."

"We're the only girls in the whole high school who aren't allowed to wear silk stockings," Ernestine complained. "It just isn't fair. If we could just wear silk stockings it wouldn't be so bad about the long skirts, the sensible shoes, and the cootie garages."

"No, by jingo." Dad pounded the table. "I'll put you both in a convent first. I will, by jingo. Silk stockings indeed! I don't want to hear another word out of either of you, or into the convent you go. Do you understand?"

The convent had become one of Dad's most frequently used threats. He had even gone so far as to write away for literature on convents, and he kept several catalogues on the tea table in the dining room, where he could thumb through them and wave them during his arguments with the older girls.

"There seems to be a nice convent near Albany," he'd tell Mother after making sure that Anne and Ernestine were listening. "The catalogue says the wall around it is twelve feet high, and the sisters see to it that the girls are in bed by nine o'clock. I think that's better than the one at Boston. The wall of the Boston one is only ten feet high."

The so-called cootie garages, which Anne and Ernestine now detested, had been the style several years before, and still were worn by girls who hadn't bobbed their hair. The long hair was pulled forward and tied into two droopy pugs which protruded three or four inches from each ear. If a girl didn't have enough hair to do the trick, she used rags, rats, or switches to fill up the insides of the ear muffs.

Anne decided that she could never get Dad's permission to dress like the other girls in her class, and that it was up to her to take matters into her own hands. She felt a certain amount of responsibility to Ernestine and the younger girls, since she knew they would never be emancipated until she paved the way. She had a haunting mental picture of Jane, fifteen years hence, still wearing pugs over her ears, long winter drawers, and heavy ribbed stockings.

"Convent, here I come," she told Ern. "I mean the Albany convent with the twelve-foot wall."

She disappeared into the girls' bathroom with a pair of scissors. When she emerged, her hair was bobbed and shingled up the back. It wasn't a very good-looking job, but it was good and short. She tiptoed, unnoticed, into Ernestine's room.

"How do I look?" she asked. "Do you think I did a good job?"

"Good Lord," Ernestine screamed. "Get out of here. It might be catching."

"I'll catch it when Dad gets ahold of me, I know that. But how does it look?"

"I didn't know any human head of hair could look like that," Ernestine said. "I like bobbed hair, but yours looks like you backed into a lawn-mower. My advice is to start all over again, and this time let the barber do it."

"You're not much help," Anne complained. "After all, I did it as much for you as for me."

"Well, don't do anything like that for me again. I'm not worth it. It's too big a sacrifice to expect you to go around like that until the end of your days, which I suspect are numbered."

"You're going to back me up, aren't you, when Dad sees it? After all, you want to bob your hair, don't you?"

"I'll back you up," said Ern, "to the hilt. But I don't want to bob my hair. I want a barber to bob it for me. What I'm wondering is who's going to back up Dad. Somebody had better be there to catch him."

"I have a feeling," Anne said, "that I'm in for a fairly disagreeable evening. Oh, well, somebody had to do it, and I'm the oldest."

They sat in Ernestine's room until supper time, and then went downstairs together. Mother was serving the plates, and dropped peas all over the tablecloth.

"Anne," she whispered. "Your beautiful hair. Oh, oh, oh. Just look at yourself."

"I have looked at myself," Anne said. "Please don't make me look at myself again. I don't want to spoil my appetite."

Mother burst into tears. "You've already spoiled mine," she sobbed.

Dad hadn't paid any attention when Anne and Ernestine entered the dining room.

"What's the trouble now?" he asked. "Can't we have a little peace and quiet around her for just one meal? All I ask is . . ." He saw Anne and choked.

"Go back upstairs and take that thing off," he roared. "And don't you ever dare to come down here looking like that again. The idea! Scaring everybody half to death and making your Mother cry. You ought to be ashamed of yourself."

"It's done, Daddy," Anne said. "I'm afraid we're all going to have to make the best of it. The moving finger bobs, and having bobbed, moves on."

"I think it looks snakey," Ern hastened to do her duty to her older sister. "And listen, Daddy, it's ever so much more efficient. It takes me ten minutes to fix these pugs in the morning, and Anne can fix her hair now in fifteen seconds."

"What hair?" Dad shouted. "She doesn't have any hair to fix."

"How could you do this to me?" Mother sobbed.

"How could she do it to an Airedale, let alone to herself or you and me?" said Dad. "The Scarlet Letter. How Hester won her 'A.' Well, I won't have it, do you understand? I want your hair grown back in and I want it grown back in fast. Do you hear me?"

Anne had tried to keep up a bold front, but the combined attack was too much and she burst into tears.

"Nobody in this family understands me," she sobbed. "I wish I were dead."

She ran from the table. We heard her bedroom door slam, and muffled, heartbroken sobs.

Dad reached over and picked up his convent catalogues, but he couldn't put any enthusiasm into them, and he finally tossed them down again. Neither he nor Mother could eat anything, and there was an uneasy, guilty silence, punctuated by Anne's sobs.

"Listen to that poor, heartbroken child," Mother finally said. "Imagine her thinking that no one in the world understands her. Frank, I think you were too hard on her."

Dad put his head in his hands. "Maybe I was," he said. "Maybe I was. Personally, I don't have anything much against bobbed hair. Like Ernestine says, it's more efficient. But when I saw how upset it made you, I lost my temper, I guess."

"I don't have anything against bobbed hair either," Mother said. "It certainly would eliminate a lot of brushing and combing. But I knew you didn't like it, and . . ."

Anne appeared at dessert time, red-eyed and disheveled. Without a word she sat down and picked up her knife and fork. Minutes later, she smiled enchantingly.

"That was good," she said, passing her plate. "If you don't mind, Mother, I'll have another helping of everything. I'm positively starved tonight."

"I don't mind, dear," said Mother.

"I like to see girls eat," said Dad.

That weekend, Mother took the girls down to Dad's barber shop in the Claridge Building in Montclair.

"I want you to trim this one's hair, please," she said, pointing to Anne, "and to bob the hair of the others."

"Any special sort of bob, Mrs. Gilbreth?" the barber asked.

"No. No, I guess just a regular bob," Mother said slowly. "The shorter the better."

"And how about you, Mrs. Gilbreth?"

"What about me?"

"How about your hair?"

"No, sir," the girls shouted indignantly. "You don't touch a hair on her head. The idea!"

Mother pretended to consider the suggestion. "I don't know, girls," she smiled. "It might look very chic. And it certainly would be more efficient. What do you think?"

"I think," said Ernestine, "it would be disgraceful. After all, a mother's a mother, not a silly flapper."

"I guess not today, thank you," Mother told the barber. "Five bobbed-haired bandits in the family should be enough."

Having capitulated on the hair question, Dad put up an even sterner resistance against any future changes in dress. But Anne and Ernestine broke him down a little at a time. Anne got a job in the high-school cafeteria, saved her money, and bought silk stockings, two short dresses and four flimsy pieces of underwear known as teddies. These she unwrapped with some ceremony in the living room.

"I don't want to be a sneak," she said, "so I'm going to show these to everybody right now. If you won't let me wear them at home, I'll change into them on the way to school. I'm never going to wear long underwear again."

"Oh no you don't," Dad shouted. "Take those things back to the store. It embarrasses me to look at them, and I won't have them in my house."

He picked up a teddy and held the top of it against his shoulders. It hung down to his belt.

"You mean that's all the underwear women wear nowadays?" he asked incredulously. "When I think of . . . well, never mind that. No wonder you read about all those crimes and love nests, like that New Brunswick preacher and the choir singer. Well, you take the whole business right back to the store."

"No," Anne insisted. "I bought these clothes with my own money and I'm going to wear them. I'm not going to be the only one in the class with long underwear and a flap in the back. It's disgusting."

"It's not so disgusting as having no back of the underwear to sew a flap on," said Dad. "I just can't believe that everybody in your class wears these teddybear, or bare-teddy things. There must be some sane parents besides your mother and me." He shook his head. But he was weakening.

"I don't see why you object to teddies," Anne said. "They don't show, you know."

"Of course they don't show, that's just the trouble. It's what does show that I'm talking about."

"There's only one other girl in high school besides Anne and me who doesn't wear teddies," Ernestine put in. "If you don't believe us, come to school and see for yourself."

"That won't be necessary," Dad blushed. "I'm willing to take your word for it."

"I should say not," said Mother.

"Aside from the possibility of being arrested for indecent exposure every time they crossed their legs or stood in a breeze," Dad muttered, "I'd think they'd die of pneumonia."

"Well, I'm glad there's one other sensible girl in school besides you two," Mother said, clutching at a straw. "She sounds like a nice girl. Do I know her?"

"I don't believe so," Ernestine whispered. "She doesn't even wear a teddy. And if you don't believe me . . ."

"I know," Dad blushed again. "And it still won't be necessary."

He picked up one of the stockings and slipped his hand into it.

"You might as well go bare-legged as to wear these. You can see right through them. It's like the last of the seven veils. And those arrows at the bottom—why do they point in that direction?"

"Those aren't arrows, Daddy," Anne said. "They're clocks. And it seems to me that you're going out of your way to find fault with them."

"Well, why couldn't the hands of the clock have stopped at quarter after three or twenty-five of five, instead of six o'clock?"

"Be sensible, Daddy," Anne begged him. "You don't want us to grow up to be wallflowers, do you?"

"I'd a lot rather raise wallflowers than clinging vines or worse. The next thing I know you'll be wanting to paint."

"Everybody uses make-up nowadays," Ern said. "They don't call it painting any more."

"I don't care what they call it," Dad roared. "I'll have no painted women in this house. Get that straight. The bare-teddies and six-o'clock stockings are all right, I guess, but no painting, do you understand?"

"Yes, Daddy."

"And no high heels or pointed toes. I'm not going to have a lot of doctor's bills because of foot troubles."

Anne and Ernestine decided that half a loaf was better than none, and that they had better wait until Dad got used to the silk stockings and short skirts before they pressed the make-up and shoe question.

But it turned out that Dad had given all the ground he intended to, and the girls found Mother a weak reed on which to lean.

"Neither my sisters nor I have ever used face powder," Mother told Anne and Ernestine, when they asked her to intervene in their behalf. "Frankly girls, I consider it non-essential."

"Don't tell me you'd rather see a nose full of freckles!"

"At least that looks natural. And when it comes to the matter of high heels, I don't see how your father can be expected to travel around the world talking about eliminating fatigue, while you girls are fatiguing yourself with high heel shoes."

Dad kept a sharp lookout for surreptitious painting, and was especially suspicious whenever one of the girls looked particularly pretty.

"What's got into you tonight?" he'd ask, sniffing the air for traces of powder or perfume.

Ernestine, after playing outside most of the afternoon, came to supper one evening with flushed cheeks.

"Come over here, young lady," Dad yelled. "I warned you about painting. Let me take a look at you. I declare, you girls pay no more attention to me than if I were a cigar store Indian. A man's got to wear grease in his hair and gray flannel trousers to get any attention in this house nowadays."

"I haven't got on makeup, Daddy."

"You haven't eh? Don't think you can fool me. And don't think I'm fooling you when I tell you you've just about painted your way into that convent."

"The one with the twelve-foot wall, or the one with the ten-foot wall?" Ern asked.

"Don't be impudent." He pulled out a handkerchief and held a corner of it out to Ern. "Spit on that."

He took the wet part of the handkerchief, rubbed her cheeks and examined it.

"Well, Ernestine," he said after a minute. "I see that it isn't rouge, and I apologize. But it might have been, and I won't have it, do you hear?"

Dad prided himself on being able to smell perfume as soon as he walked into a room, and on being able to pick the offender out of a crowd.

"Ernestine, are you the one we have to thank for that smell?" he asked. "Good Lord. It smells like a French . . . like a French garbage can."

"What smell, Daddy?"

"By jingo, don't tell me you're indulging in perfume now!"

"Why not, Daddy? Perfume isn't painting or make-up. And it smells so good!"

"Why not? Because it stinks up good fresh air, that's why not. Now go up and wash that stuff off before I come up and wash it off for you. Don't you know what men think when they smell perfume on a woman?"

"All I know is what one man thinks," Ernestine complained. "And he thinks I should wash it off."

"Thinks, nothing," said Dad. "He knows. And he's telling you. Now get moving."

Clothes remained a subject of considerable friction, but the matter that threatened to affect Dad's stability was jazz. Radios were innocuous, being still in the catwhisker and headphone stage, and featuring such stimulating programs as the Arlington Time Signals. But five- and six-piece dance bands were turning out huge piles of graphophone records, and we tried to buy them all.

We already had an ample supply of graphophones, because of the ones Dad had acquired for the language records. And we still weren't allowed to neglect our language lessons. But once we had played the required quota of French, German, and Italian records, we switched to "Stumbling," "Limehouse Blues," "Last Night on the Back Porch," "Charlie, My Boy," "I'm Forever Blowing Bubbles," and "You've Got to See Mama Every Night or You Can't See Mama at All." Not only did we listen to them, we sang with them, imitated them, and rolled back the rugs and danced to them.

Dad didn't particularly object to jazz music. He thought some of it was downright catchy. But he felt that we devoted far too much time to it, that the words were something more than suggestive, and that the kind of dancing that went with it might lead to serious consequences. As he walked from room to room in the house, jazz assailed him from phonograph after phonograph, and he sometimes threw up his hands in disgust.

"Da-da, de-da-da-da," he bellowed sarcastically. "If you spent half as much time improving your minds as you do memorizing those stupid songs, you could recite *The Koran* forwards and backwards. Wind up the victrola and let's have some more jazz. Da-da, de-da-da-da. Let's have that record about 'I love my sweetie a hundred times a night.' "

"You made that song up," we told him. "That's not a record, Daddy."

"Maybe it's not a record," he said. "But take it from me, it's well above average. Da-da, de-da-da-da."

When Anne came home from school one afternoon and announced that she had been invited to her first dance, she seemed so happy that both Dad and Mother were happy for her.

"I told you that if I started dressing like the other girls everything would be all right and that I would be popular with the boys," Anne crowed. "Joe Scales has asked me to go with him to the prom next Friday night."

"That's lovely, dear," Mother said.

"That's just fine," Dad smiled. "Is he a nice boy?"

"Nice? Gee, I'll say. He's a cheerleader and he has a car."

"Two mighty fine recommendations," Dad said. "If only he had a raccoon coat I suppose he'd be listed in the year book as the one most likely to succeed."

The sarcasm was lost on Anne. "He's going to get his raccoon coat next year when he goes to Yale," she hastened to assure Dad. "His father's promised it to him if he passes his work."

"That takes a load off my mind," said Dad. "It used to be that a father promised his son a gold watch if he didn't smoke until he was twenty-one. Now the kids get a raccoon coat as a matter of routine if they manage to stumble through high school."

He shook his head and sighed. "Honestly, I don't know what the world's coming to," he said. "I really don't. Friday night, you say?" He pulled a notebook out of his pocket and consulted it. "It's all right. I can make it."

"You can make what?" Anne asked him suspiciously.

"I can make the dance," said Dad. "You didn't think for a minute I was going to let you go out by yourself, at night, with that—that cheerleader, did you?"

"Oh, Daddy," Anne moaned. "You wouldn't spoil everything by doing something like that, would you? What's he going to think of me?"

"He'll think you're a sensible, well-brought-up child, with sensible parents," Mother put in. "I'm sure that if I called up his mother right now, she'd be glad to hear that your father was going along as a chaperone."

"Don't you trust your own flesh and blood?"

"Of course we trust you," Dad said. "I know you've been brought up right. I trust all my daughters. It's that cheerleader I don't trust. Now you might as well make up your mind to it. Either I go, or you don't."

"Do you think it would help if I called up his mother and explained the situation to her?" Mother asked.

Anne had become philosophic about breaking Dad down a little at a time, and she had suspected all along that there was going to be a third person on her first date.

"No, thanks, Mother," she said. "I'd better announce the news myself, in my own way. I guess I'll have to tell him about some people still being in the dark concerning the expression that two's company and three's a crowd. I don't know what he's going to say, though."

"He'll probably be tickled to death to have someone along to pay for the sodas," Dad told her.

"Shall I tell him we'll go in his car, or ours?" Anne asked.

"His car? I haven't seen it, but I can imagine it. No doors, no fenders, no top, and a lot of writing about in case of fire throw this in. I wouldn't be seen dead in it, even if the dance was a masquerade and I was going as a cheerleader. No sir. We'll go in Foolish Carriage."

"Sometimes," Anne said slowly, "it's hard to be the oldest. When I think of Ernestine, Martha, Lillian, Jane—they won't have to go through any of this. I wonder if they'll just take things for granted, or whether they'll appreciate what I've suffered for them."

On the night of Anne's first date, we stationed ourselves at strategic windows so we could watch Joe Scales arrive. It wasn't every day that a cheerleader came to call.

As Dad had predicted, Anne's friend drove up to the house in an ancient Model T, with writing on it. We could hear the car several blocks before it actually hove into sight, because it was equipped with an exhaust whistle that was allowed to function as a matter of routine. When the car proceeded at a moderate speed, which was hardly ever, the whistle sounded no worse than an hellish roar. But when young Mister Scales stepped on the gas, the roar became high pitched, deafening, and insane.

As the Model T bumped down Eagle Rock Way, heads popped out of the windows of neighboring houses, dogs raced into the woods with their tails between their legs, and babies started to scream.

The exhaust whistle, coupled with the natural engine noises, precluded the necessity of Mister Scales' giving any further notice about the car's arrival at its destination. But etiquette of the day was rigid, and he followed it to the letter. First he turned off the engine, which automatically and mercifully silenced the whistle. Then, while lounging in the driver's seat, he tooted and re-tooted the horn until Anne finally came to the front door.

"Come on in, Joe," Anne called.

"Okay, baby. Is your pop ready?"

Dad was peeking at the arrival from behind a curtain in his office. "If he 'pops' me, I'll pop him," Dad whispered to Mother. "My God, Lillie. I mean, Great Caesar's ghost. Come here and look at him. It's Joe College in the flesh. And he just about comes up to Anne's shoulder."

Anne's sheik was wearing a black-and-orange-striped blazer, gray Oxford bags, a bow tie on an elastic band, and a brown triangular porkpie hat, pinched into a bowsprit at the front.

"You and I are going to the dance," Joe shouted to Anne, "And so's your Old Man. Get it? So's your Old Man."

"Of course she gets it, wise guy," Dad grumbled for Mother's benefit. "What do you think she is, a moron? And let me hear you refer to me tonight as the 'Old Man' and you'll get it, too. I promise you."

"Hush," Mother warned him, coming over to peek out the curtain. "He'll hear you. Actually, he's kind of cute, in a sort of vest-pocket way."

"Cute?" said Dad. "He looks like what might happen if a pigmy married a barber pole. And look at that car. What's that written on the side? 'Jump in sardine, here's your tin.'"

"Well don't worry about the car," Mother told him. "You'll be riding in yours, not that contraption."

"Thank the Lord for small favors. You stall him and Anne off until I can get the side curtains put up. I'm not going to drive through town with that blazer showing. Someone might think he was one of our kids."

Dad disappeared in the direction of the barn, and Mother went into the living room to meet the caller. As she entered, Joe was demonstrating to Frank and Bill how the bow tie worked.

"It's a William Tell tie," he said, holding the bow away from his neck and allowing it to pop back into position. "You pull the bow and it hits the apple."

Both Frank and Bill were impressed.

"You're the first cheerleader we ever saw up close," Frank said. "Gee."

Joe was sitting down when he was introduced to Mother. Remembering his manners, he tipped his hat, unveiling for just a moment a patent-leather hairdo, parted in the middle.

"Will you lead some cheers for us?" Bill begged. "We know them all. Anne and Ernestine taught them to us."

Joe leaped to his feet. "Sure thing," he said. He cupped his hands over his mouth and shouted in an adolescent baritone that cracked and made Mother shudder:

"Let's have a hoo, rah, ray and a tiger for Montclair High. A hoo, rah, ray and a tiger. I want to hear you holler now. Readddy?"

He turned sideways to us, dropped on one knee and made his fists go in a circle, like a squirrel on a treadmill.

"Hoo," he screamed, at the top of his voice. "Rah. Ray . . ."

It was at this point that Dad entered the room. He stood viewing the proceedings with disgust, lips pursed and hands on hips. At the end of the cheer, he sidled over toward Mother.

"The car won't start," he whispered, "and I can't say that I blame it. What shall I do?"

"You could go in his car."

"With that insane calliope and those signs?" Dad hissed. "Do I look like a sardine looking for a tin to leap into?"

"Not exactly," Mother conceded. "Why don't you call a cab, then?"

"Look at him," Dad whispered. "He doesn't come up to her shoulder. He wouldn't dare get funny with her—she'd knock him cold."

Dad walked over to where Joe and Anne were sitting.

"I hope you youngsters won't mind," he said, "but I won't be able to go to the dance with you."

"No, we don't mind at all, Daddy," said Anne. "Do we Joe?"

"A hoo, rah, ray and a tiger for me, is that it?" Dad asked.

Joe made no attempt to hide his elation. "That's it," he said. "Come on, baby. Let's shake that thing. We're running late."

"Now I want you to be home at midnight," Dad said to Anne. "I'm going to be right here waiting for you, and if you're not here by one minute after midnight I'm coming looking for you. Do you understand?"

"All right, Daddy," Anne grinned. "Good old Foolish Carriage saved the day, didn't it?"

"That," said Dad, "and the way certain other matters"—he looked pointedly down at Scales—"shaped up."

"Come on, Cinderella," said Scales, "before the good fairy turns things into field mice and pumpkins."

He and Anne departed, and he didn't forget to tip his hat.

"Do you guess he meant me?" Dad asked Mother. "Why the little . . . I ought to break his neck."

"Of course not. He was speaking in generalities, I'm sure."

The hellish whistle could be heard gradually disappearing in the distance.

CHAPTER 18

Motorcycle Mac

ONCE the ice was broken, Anne started having dates fairly often, and Ernestine and Martha followed suit. Dad acted as chaperone whenever the pressure of business permitted. Although he had decided that Joe Scales was small enough to be above suspicion, he had no confidence in the football heroes and other sheiks who soon were pitching their tents and woo upon the premises. When Dad couldn't act as chaperone himself, he sent Frank or Bill along as his proxy.

"It's bad enough to have you tagging along on a date," Ernestine told Dad. "But to have a kid brother squirming and giggling on the back seat is simply unbearable. I don't know why the boys in school bother with us."

"Well, I know, even if you don't," Dad said. "And that's exactly why Frank and Bill are there. And let me tell you, if those sheiks would stop bothering you and find some other desert to haunt, it would suit me just right."

Frank and Bill didn't like the chaperone job any more than the girls liked having them for chaperones.

"For Lord's sake, Daddy," Frank complained, "I feel just like a third wheel sitting in the back seat all by myself."

"That's just what you're supposed to be—the third wheel. I don't expect you to be able to thrash those fullbacks if they start trying to take liberties with your sisters. But at least you'll be able to run for help."

The girls complained to Mother, but as usual she sided with Dad.

"If you ask me," Anne told her, "it's a dead give away to be as suspicious as Daddy. It denotes a misspent youth."

"Well nobody asked you," Mother said, "so perhaps you'd better forego any further speculation. It's not a case of suspicion. Just because other parents won't face up to their responsibilities is no reason for your father or me to forget ours."

At the dances, Dad would sit by himself against a wall, as far away from the orchestra as possible, and work on papers he had brought along in a brief case. At first no one paid much attention to him, figuring perhaps that if he was ignored he might go away. But after a few months he was accepted as a permanent fixture, and the girls and boys went out of their way to speak to him and bring him refreshments. People, even sheiks, couldn't be around Daddy without liking him. And Daddy couldn't be in the midst of people without being charming.

"Do you see what's happening?" Anne whispered to Ernestine one night, pointing to the crowd around Dad's chair. "By golly, he's become the belle of the high school ball. What do you think of that?"

"I think it's a pain in the neck," Ernestine said. "But it's kind of cute, isn't it?"

"Not only cute, it's our salvation. You wait and see."

"What do you mean?"

"When Daddy gets to know the boys, and sees that they're pretty good kids, he'll decide this chaperone business is a waste of time. He really hates being here, away from Mother. And if he can find a way to quit gracefully, he'll quit."

Dad resigned as chaperone the next day, at Sunday dinner.

"I'm all through wet nursing you," he told the girls. "If you want to go to the dogs—or at any rate to the tea hounds—you're going to have to go by yourselves from now on. I can't take any more of it."

"They're really not bad kids, are they Daddy?" Anne grinned.

"Bad kids? How do I know whether they're bad kids? Naturally they behave when I'm around. But that's not the point. The point is they're making a character out of me. They're setting me up as the meddlesome but harmless old duffer, a kind of big-hearted, well-meaning, asinine, mental eunuch. The boys slap me on the back and the girls pinch me on my cheek and ask me to dance with them. If there's anything I hate, it's a Daddy-Long-Legs kind of father like that."

He turned to Mother.

"I know it's not your fault, Boss, but things would have been a whole lot easier if we had had all boys, like I suggested, instead of starting out with the girls."

From that day on, about the only contact Dad had with the sheiks was over the telephone.

"Some simpleton with pimples in his voice wants to speak to Ernestine," he grumbled to Mother when he answered the phone. "I'll swear, I'm going to have that instrument taken out of here. These tea hounds are running me crazy. I wish they'd sniff around someone else's daughters for awhile, and give us some peace."

Libby Holton, one of the girls in Anne's class, was from Mississippi and had only recently moved with her family to Montclair. She was pretty, mature for her age, and even the straight silhouette styles couldn't hide her figure. She was a heavy painter and wore the highest heels and the shortest skirts in the school. She looked like everything Dad said his daughters shouldn't look like.

Libby was charming and popular. She and Anne became good friends, and Anne finally had her over for lunch. Libby's place was next to Dad's, and she was loaded with perfume—you could smell it the minute she walked into the house. Knowing how Dad disliked make-up and perfume, we were afraid he was going to make Anne's friend change her place at the table or, worse still, order her to go upstairs and wash herself.

We might have saved ourselves the worry, because it soon became apparent that while Dad didn't like perfume on his own daughters, he didn't object to it on other people's daughters.

"My, that smells good," he told Libby after he had been introduced. "I'm glad you're going to sit right here next to me, where I can keep an eye and a nose on you."

"Why, I declare," said Libby. "Anne Gilbreth, you hussy you, why didn't you tell me you had such a gallant Daddy? And so handsome, too."

"Oh, boy," groaned Bill.

Libby turned to Bill and dropped him a slow, fluttering wink. "Ain't I the limit?" she laughed.

"Oh, boy," said Bill. But this time it was more of a yodel than a groan.

Both Anne and Libby worked hard on Dad all during lunch. He saw through them, but he enjoyed it. He imitated Libby's southern accent, called her Honey Chile and You-All, and outdid himself telling stories and jokes.

"I heard from some of the other girls in school about how cute you were," said Libby. "They said the nicest things about you. And they said you used to come to all the dances, too."

"That's right. And if I had known about the Mississippi invasion I would have started going to the dances all over again."

After dessert, we sat around the table wondering what came next. We knew, and so did Dad, that it was a build up for something. Just as Dad finally pushed back his chair, Anne cleared her throat.

"You know, Daddy, there's something I've been wanting to ask you for a long time."

"And now, having been flattered, fattened, and fussed over, the sucker is led forward for the shake-down," Dad grinned. "Well, speak up girls. What is it?"

"Why don't you take this afternoon off and teach Libby and me how to drive the car? We're almost old enough to get licenses, and it would be a big convenience for the whole family if someone besides you knew how to drive."

"Is that all? You didn't need all the sweet-talk for that. I thought you were going to ask me to let you spend the weekend at Coney Island or something." He looked at his watch. "I'm going to have to put some more Neatsfoot oil on the clutch. I'll have the car out front in exactly twelve minutes."

Libby and Anne both threw their arms around his neck.

"I never thought he'd do it," Anne said.

"I told you he'd say yes," Libby grinned. "Mr. Gilbreth, you're a sweet old duck." She planted a kiss on his cheek, leaving two red, lipsticked smears.

The girls rushed out of the dining room to get ready, and Dad rolled his eyes.

"Well, Lillie," he said to Mother, "I guess my spring chicken days are over. When you start getting pecks on the cheek from your daughters' friends, you're on the decline."

"The first thing I know you'll be greasing your hair and wearing one of those yellow slickers," Mother admonished him with mock severity. "Better wash the lipstick off your face before you go out, sheik."

Dad grinned vacantly, and walked so that his pants cuffs swished like Oxford bags.

"I'm going out and take the fenders off Foolish Carriage," he said. "Four Wheels, No Brakes. The Tin You Love to Touch."

Frank, Bill and Lillian, still in junior high school, resented the infiltration of the high school romeos. What they objected to principally was that the three oldest girls were being turned away from family activities. Anne, Ernestine, and Martha had less and less time for family games, for plays, and skits. It was the inevitable prelude to growing up. It was just a few bars, if you please, professor, of that sentimental little ditty entitled "Those Wedding Bells Are Breaking up That Old Gang of Mine." Marriage was still in the distant future, but the stage was being set.

Anne already had had her first proposal. Joe Scales had asked her to marry him. They were sitting in a hammock on the side porch when he popped the question. The porch was separated by French doors from the parlor and by windows from the office. Frank, Bill and Lillian, lying flat on the parlor floor and peeking through the doors, bore witness to the proposal and to Anne's none-too-original rejection.

"I like to think of you as a brother," she told Scales.

"A fine thing!" Frank whispered to Bill. "Imagine thinking of that wet smack in terms of us."

"You caught me," Scales told Anne. "I went for you, hook, line and sinker. What are you going to do with me?"

Anne was touched by this show of slavish devotion. "What am I going to do with you?" she echoed dramatically.

"Throw him back," Dad roared from the other side of the office window. "He's too small to keep."

Frank, Bill and Lill fought gamely against the invasion, but in vain. More effective, although unpremeditated, were the obstacles erected by the four little boys, Fred, Dan, Jack, and Bob, who kept running in and out of the rooms where the older girls were entertaining their callers.

"I'm living through what can only be described as a hell on earth," Anne moaned to Mother. "It's impossible to entertain at home with that troop of four berserk little boys. Something drastic has got to be done about them."

"What's the matter with them?"

"They're in and out of the porch all evening. Up in my lap, up in my friend's lap, under the hammock, over the hammock, in and out, up and down, over and under, until I'm about to go daft."

"Well, what do you suggest, dear?"

"Tie them down."

At the end of one particular evening, Anne became almost hysterical.

"I'm fed up to the eyeballs with that button brigade," she sobbed. "They're driving me screaming, screeching mad. How can you expect any boy to get into a romantic mood when you have to button and unbutton all evening?"

"They're not supposed to get into romantic moods," Dad said. "That's just what we don't want around here."

Anne paid no attention to him. "It's 'Andy, unbutton me, I have to get undressed.' It's 'Andy button me up, I'm cold.' It's 'Andy, its three o'clock in the button factory.' I tell you, Mother, its just too much of a handicap to endure. You're going to have to do something about it, unless you want all your daughters to be old maids."

"You're right," Mother conceded. "I'll do my best to keep them upstairs the next time you have company. I wonder what four sets of leg irons would cost?"

The opposition of Frank, Bill and Lill was less subtle.

"You want to speak to Martha?" Frank would say in an incredulous voice when one of her sheiks would telephone. "You're absolutely sure? You haven't got her mixed up with somebody else? You mean Martha Gilbreth, the one with all the freckles? Oh, mercy! Don't hang up, please. Are you still there? Thank goodness! Please don't hang up."

Then, holding the telephone so that the boy on the other end could still hear him, Frank would shout desperately:

"Martha, come quick. Imagine! It's a boy calling for you. Isn't that wonderful? Hurry up. He might hang up."

"Give me that phone, you little snake-in-the-grass," Martha would scream in a white rage. "When I get through I'll tear your eyes out, you unspeakable little brat, you." And then, in a honeyed voice, into the mouthpiece. "Helloooo. Who? Well, good looking, where have you been all my life? You have? Well, I've been waiting too. Uh, huh."

One of Ernestine's admirers was shy and subdued, and never could bring himself to tell her what he thought of her. After he had been calling on her for almost a year, he finally mustered his courage and had a beautiful picture taken of himself. Then he inscribed across the bottom of the picture, in purple ink, a very special message.

The message said, "All My Fondest Thoughts Are of You, Dearest Ernestine."

He couldn't bring himself to give the picture to her personally, so he wrapped it up, insured it for one hundred dollars, and sent it through the mail.

Ern kept it hidden in a bureau drawer, but no hiding place in our house was any too safe, and the junior-high-school contingent finally discovered it, memorized it, put it to music, and learned a three-part harmony for it.

The next time the bashful boy came to call, Frank, Bill and Lill, hidden in a closet under the front steps, started to sing:

"All my fondest thoughts,

"(My fondest thoughts)

"Are of you,

"(Yes, nobody else but you)

"My Dearest Ernestine,

"(I don't mean Anne; I don't mean Mart)

"But Dearest Ernestine."

The shrinking sheik turned a bright crimson and actually cringed against the hatrack, while Ernestine picked up one of Dad's walking sticks and started after the younger set, bent on premeditated, cold-blooded mayhem.

As a matter of routine, Frank and Bill would answer the front door when a sheik came to call and subject him to a preliminary going over, designed to make him feel ill at ease for the balance of the evening.

"Look at the suit," Frank would say, opening the coat and examining the inside label. "I thought so. Larkey's Boys Store. Calling all lads to Larkeys. College-cut clothes, with two pairs of trousers, for only seventeen fifty. This fellow's a real sport, all right."

"Pipe the snakey socks," Bill would say, lifting up the sheik's pant leg. "Green socks and a blue tie. And yellow shoes."

"You kids cut it out or I'll knock you into the middle of next week," the sheik would protest hopelessly. "Have a heart, will you? Beat it now, and tell your sister I'm here."

Frank brought out a folding ruler that he had slipped into his pocket a few minutes before, and measured the cuffs of the visitor's pants.

"Twenty-three inches," Frank told Bill. "That's collegiate, all right, but it's two inches less collegiate than the cuffs of Anne's sheik. Let's see that tie . . ."

"Let's see his underwear," Bill suggested.

"Hey, stop that," the sheik protested. "Get your hands off of me. Go tell your sister that I'm here, now, or there's going to be trouble."

One of Ernestine's sheiks drove a motorcycle madly around town, and used to buzz our place three or four times a night in hopes of catching sight of her. Mother and Dad didn't allow the boys to come calling on school nights, but there was always a chance Ernestine might be out in the yard or standing by a window.

One night he parked his motorcycle a couple of blocks away, crept up to the house, and climbed a cherry tree near Ernestine's bedroom window. Fortunately for the motorcyclist, Dad was out of town on business.

Ernestine was doing her homework, and had a spooky feeling she was being watched through the open window. It suddenly occurred to her that she hadn't heard the motorcycle go chugging by the house for several hours, and she immediately grew suspicious.

She walked into a dark room, peeked out from behind a shade, and saw the sheik high up in the cherry tree silhouetted against the moon. She was furious.

"The sneaking peeping tom," she told Anne. "Good golly, I was just about to get undressed. There's no telling what he might have seen, if I hadn't had that creepy feeling I was being watched."

"The sight probably would have toppled him right out of the tree," Anne said a little sarcastically. "Do you think he knows you saw him?"

"I don't know, but I don't think so."

"Come on, we'll peek out that dark window again," Anne said. "If he's still there, I've got an idea."

He was still there, and Anne quickly rounded up Martha, Frank, Bill, and Lillian.

"There's a peeping tom in the cherry tree," Anne explained. "One of Ernestine's. He needs to be taught a lesson. If he gets away with it and tells the other boys around school, our cherry trees are going to look like the bleachers at the Polo Grounds."

"It would certainly play hob with the crop," Frank said.

"Now, not a word to Mother," Anne continued, "because she'll play her part better if she doesn't know what's going on. Ernestine, go back into your room and tease him along. Don't pull down your shades. Comb your hair, take off your shoes and socks. Even fiddle around with the buttons on your dress, if you want to. Anything to keep him interested. The rest of you, come with me."

We went down into the cellar, where Anne took some wire and fastened a rag to the end of a stick. The rest of us loaded our arms with old newspapers, excelsior and packing boxes. Then outside Anne poured kerosene over the rag, lighted it, and led a torch parade from the cellar toward the cherry tree.

Ern's sheik was so interested in what seemed about to transpire in her bedroom that he didn't notice us at first. But as the parade drew closer, he looked down. We formed a ring around the base of the tree, and one by one deposited our combustibles at the trunk. As the pile of refuse grew, Anne swung her torch closer and closer to it.

"Christmas," the peeping tom shouted in terror. "Are you trying to burn me to the stake? Don't set fire to that. You'll roast me alive."

"Precisely," said Anne. "Precisely what you deserve, too. If you know any prayers, start babbling them."

"It was just a prank," he pleaded. "Just a boyish prank, that's all. Watch out for that torch. Let me come down. I'll go quietly."

"Let you come down, nothing," said Martha. "You evil-minded thing you. Let you come down and spread the story all over town about how you climbed our cherry tree and put one over on the Gilbreth family? I should say not."

Anne swung the torch nearer the pile of refuse.

"Look out," the peeping tom shrieked. "You wouldn't roast me alive in cold blood, would you? By God, I believe you would!"

"Of course we would," Frank said. "Dead men tell no tales."

Ernestine stuck her head out of the window.

"Have you got him trapped?" she called. "Good. I've been fiddling with the buttons on my dress so long I'm about to wear all the skin off the tips of my fingers. Is he who I think he is?"

"None other," said Anne. "Motorcycle Mac himself, in the soon-to-be-seared flesh. Treed like a tree toad in a tree."

"Don't cremate him until I get down there," Ernestine begged. "I want to see the fun."

Motorcycle Mac was alternately whimpering and cursing when Ernestine joined the ring around the cherry tree.

"I always thought he was a nasty boy anyway," Ernestine said. "Sheiks are hard to find, and goodness knows I don't have too many of them. But he's one I'll be glad to sacrifice."

"I don't blame you," said Martha. "He's a particularly disagreeable one, all right. He's even a cry baby. I hope when it comes my time to cash in my chips I'll be able to go out with a trace of a smile on my beautiful lips, like Wally Reid."

"Yes," said Anne. "I have the feeling that if anyone has to be cremated, it couldn't happen to a more objectionable sheik."

We had counted on the commotion to attract Mother's attention, and now she opened her window and put her head out.

"What in the world's going on out there?" she called. "What are you doing with that torch? Which one of you is swinging it? That doesn't look safe to me, children."

"I have it," Anne said. "It's all right, Mother. We've trapped a skunk up in the cherry tree, and we're trying to make him come down."

Mother sniffed the air suspiciously.

"I thought I smelled something," she said. "Now listen, children, I don't think you ought to burn up that cherry tree for any old skunk. Your father is devoted to that tree, and he's devoted to cherry pie. Just come on in the house, and let's see if the skunk won't come down and go away by itself."

"Oh, we weren't really going to burn the tree," Ernestine giggled. "We just wanted to scare hell out of the skunk."

"Ernestine, I forbid that kind of Eskimo language," Mother said, in a shocked tone. "Now I think you'd better come into the house, all of you. It's bedtime, and even a skunk is entitled to some peace and quiet. You've scared him enough for one night. I'll bet his eyes are about to pop out of his head with what he's seen tonight."

Mother disappeared inside the window.

"I'll bet," Ernestine said for the benefit of Motorcycle Mac, "that his eyes were about to pop out of his head with what he *thought* he was going to see. Now slink down out of that cherry tree, you rat you."

"If Dad were here," Bill said, "he'd probably blind him, like they did back in Lady Godiva's day."

"That's just what Dad would do," Anne agreed. "I wish we had thought of that ourselves."

"Should I go get a hatpin?" Frank asked hopefully.

"Too late now," Anne said. "It's past your bedtime. But maybe he'll come back again some other night."

CHAPTER 19

The Party Who Called You . . .

NONE of us children knew it, but Dad had had a bad heart for years, and now Dr. Burton told him he was going to die.

We noticed that Dad had grown thinner. For the first time in twenty-five years he weighed less than two hundred pounds. He joked about how strange it was to be able to see his feet again. His hands had begun to tremble a little and his face was gray. Sometimes, when he was playing baseball with the older boys or rolling on the floor with Bob and Jane, he'd stop suddenly and say he guessed he had had enough for today. There was a trace of a stagger as he walked away.

He was fifty-five years old, and we supposed his symptoms were those of approaching old age. Certainly it never occurred to any of us that Dad had any intention of dying until he was good and ready to die.

231

He had known about the bad heart even before Bob and Jane were born. He and Mother had discussed it, and the possibility that she would be left a widow with all the children.

"But I don't think those doctors know what they're talking about," Dad said.

Mother knew the answer Dad wanted.

"I don't see how twelve children would be much more trouble than ten," she told him, "and personally I like to finish what I start. I don't know about you."

The bad heart was one of the principal reasons for Dad's home instruction programs. It was also why he had organized the house on an efficiency basis, so that it would operate smoothly without supervision; so that the older children would be responsible for the younger ones. He knew a load was going to be thrown on Mother, and he wanted to lessen it as much as he could.

"Maybe tomorrow, maybe in six months," Dr. Burton told Dad now. "A year at the outside if you stop work and stay in bed."

"Don't think you can scare me," Dad said. "You doctors have been telling me for three years not to subscribe to any new magazines. Well, I don't believe a word of it. For one thing, I'm in my prime. And for another, I'm too busy."

"Still the Old Pioneer," Dr. Burton grinned.

"Don't think you can scare me," Dad repeated. "I'll be in the amen corner when they're laying you away. I'll see you in church, even if you don't see me."

Dad went home and wrote a letter to a friend, Miss Myrtell Canavan, the Boston brain specialist.

"Dear Mortuary Myrt: If and when I die, I'd like my brain to go to Harvard, where they are doing those brain experiments you told me about. I'd like you to handle the details. My hat size is seven and three-eighths, in case you want to get a jar ready. Don't think this letter means I'm getting ready to go any time soon, because I'm not. I'll leave a copy of this where Lillie will see it when the time comes, and she'll get in touch with you. The next time I see you, I don't want you casting any appraising glances at my cranium."

With the letter mailed, Dad shrugged thoughts of death out of his mind. The World Power Conference and the International Management Conference were going to meet in eight months in England and Czechoslovakia, respectively. Dad accepted invitations to speak at both.

The post-war industrial expansion had resulted in more and more emphasis being placed on motion study. For the first time, both Dad and Mother had more clients than they could handle. Dad went from factory to factory, installing his time-saving systems, reducing worker fatigue, so as to speed up production.

He died on June 14, 1924, three days before he was to sail for Europe for the two conferences.

Dad had walked from our house down to the Lackawanna Station, a distance of about a mile, where he intended to catch a commuters' train for New York. He had a few minutes before the train left, and he telephoned home to Mother from a pay booth in the station.

"Say, Boss," he said, "on the way down here I had an idea about saving motions on packing those soapflakes for Lever Brothers. See what you think. . . ."

Mother heard a thud and the line went silent. She jiggled the receiver hook.

"I'm sorry," it was the voice of the operator. "The party who called you has hung up."

Jane, the baby, was two years old. Anne, the oldest, was taking her examinations at Smith, where she was a sophomore.

It was Saturday morning. The younger children were playing in the yard. Most of the older ones, members of the purchasing committees, were in town doing the marketing. Six or seven neighbors set out in automobiles to round up those who were missing. The neighbors wouldn't say what the trouble was.

"Your mother wants you home, dear," they told each of us. "There's been an accident. Just slide into the car and I'll drive you home."

When we arrived at the front of the house, we knew the accident was death. Fifteen or twenty cars were parked in the driveway and on the front lawn. Mother? It couldn't be Mother, because they had said Mother wanted us home. Daddy? Accidents didn't happen to Daddy. Somebody fell off his bicycle and was run over? Maybe. All the girls were terrible bicycle riders. Bill was a good rider but took too many chances.

We jumped out of the car and ran toward the house. Jackie was sitting on a terrace near the sidewalk. His face was smudged where he had rubbed his hands.

"Our Daddy's dead," he sobbed.

Dad was a part of all of us, and a part of all of us died then.

They dressed him in his Army uniform, and we went in and looked in the coffin. With his eyes closed and his face gone slack, he seemed stern and almost forbidding. There was no repose there and no trace left of the laugh wrinkles at the corners of his eyes.

We thought that when they came after him, Daddy must have given them a real fight. We bet they had their hands full with Daddy.

Mother found the carbon of the letter to Dad's friend, and the brain went to Harvard. After the cremation, Mother chartered a boat and went out into the Atlantic. Somewhere out there, standing alone in the bow, she scattered his ashes. That was the way Dad wanted it.

There was a change in Mother after Dad died. A change in looks and a change in manner. Before her marriage, all Mother's decisions had been made by her parents. After the marriage, the decisions were made by Dad. It was Dad who suggested having a dozen children, and that both of them become efficiency experts. If his interests had been in basket weaving or phrenology, she would have followed him just as readily.

While Dad lived, Mother was afraid of fast driving, of airplanes, of walking alone at night. When there was lightning, she went in a dark closet and held her ears. When things went wrong at dinner, she sometimes burst into tears and had to leave the table. She made public speeches, but she dreaded them.

Now, suddenly, she wasn't afraid any more, because there was nothing to be afraid of. Now nothing could upset her because the thing that mattered most had been upset. None of us ever saw her weep again.

It was two days after Dad's death, and the house still smelled of flowers. Mother called a meeting of the Family Council. It seemed natural now for her to sit at Dad's place in the chairman's chair, with a pitcher of ice water at her right.

Mother told us that there wasn't much money—most of it had

gone back into the business. She said she had talked by telephone with her mother, and that her mother wanted all of us to move out to California.

Anne interrupted to say she planned to leave college anyway and get a job. Ernestine, who had graduated from high school the night before Dad died, said she didn't care anything about college either.

"Please wait until I'm finished," Mother said, and there was a new note of authority in her voice. "There is another alternative, but it hinges on your being able to take care of yourselves. And it would involve some sacrifices from all of us. So I want you to make the decision.

"I can go ahead with your father's work. We can keep the office open here. We can keep the house, but we would have to let the cook go."

"Tom, too?" we asked. "We couldn't let Tom go, could we? He wouldn't go anyway."

"No, not Tom. But we would have to sell the car and live very simply. Still we could be together. And Anne would go back to college. You know your father wants all of you to go to college.

"Do you want to try it? Can you run the house and take care of things until I get back?"

"Get back from where, Mother?" we asked.

"If you want to try it here," she told us, and she actually rapped the table, "I'm going on that boat tomorrow; the one your father planned to take. He had the tickets. I'm going to give those speeches for him in London and Prague, by jingo. I think that's the way your father wants it. But the decision is up to you."

Ernestine and Martha went upstairs to help Mother pack. Anne disappeared into the kitchen to plan supper. Frank and Bill started down town to see the used car dealers about selling the automobile.

"Better tell them to bring a tow car," Lill called after the boys. "Foolish Carriage never starts for anybody but Daddy."

Someone once asked Dad: "But what do you want to save time *for*? What are you going to do with it?"

"For work, if you love that best," said Dad. "For education, for beauty, for art, for pleasure." He looked over the top of his pince-nez. "For mumblety-peg, if that's where your heart lies."

CHAPTER 20

And Many Years Later

SINCE the days of the stories retold in this book and its sequel, *Belles on Their Toes,* the Gilbreths have grown up, multiplied, and, like so many families, scattered—to California, Washington, New Hampshire, and places in between. Each of the boys selected a different college and entered a different field of work. All the children are married (none divorced) and have children of their own. Yet this family of individualists remains as closely knit as ever:

Mother is still carrying on our father's work. She spends much of her time working with management organizations in this country and all over the world. Yet she also finds time to visit with various members of the family and keep in touch with all we are doing. There are twenty-nine grandchildren and eleven great-grandchildren now. When she is not traveling, she lives in Montclair, works in New York, vacations in Nantucket.

Anne lives in Palo Alto, California. Her husband, Dr. Robert E. Barney, practiced dermatology in Cleveland before his retirement. They have three sons. Robert Jr. graduated from the University of California at Berkeley and is project engineer and operations planner at Herrick Iron Works in Hayward, California; he has a son, Robert Chester, and a daughter, Susan Elizabeth. Frank Gilbreth Barney, also a Berkeley alumnus, is associated with E. F. Hutton and Company in Los Angeles; he has two sons, Frank Bradford and William James. Peter Charles Barney graduated from Stanford University. He is unmarried and teaches school in Palo Alto.

Anne attended Smith College for two years and received her degree from the University of Michigan. She is occupied with family, book reviewing, and volunteer activities.

Mary died of diphtheria when she was six years old. Martha's Mary Elizabeth is named for her.

Ernestine lives in Scottsdale, Arizona. Her husband, Charles Everett Carey, is a marketing representative for Sperry Phoenix Company. Son Charles Everett Carey Jr. attends the University of Arizona. Daughter Lillian Gilbreth Carey (now Mrs. Henry Clay Clark III) has a son, Bradley Barron, and a daughter, Christine Carey. The Clarks live in Tucson, where Henry is doing graduate work in vocational rehabilitation counseling.

Ernestine, after graduation from Smith College, was a leading New York department-store buyer. She now devotes her time to family, writing, and lecturing.

Martha lives in Chehalis, Washington. Her husband, Richard Elmer Tallman, is secretary-treasurer of Hemphill-O'Neill Lumber

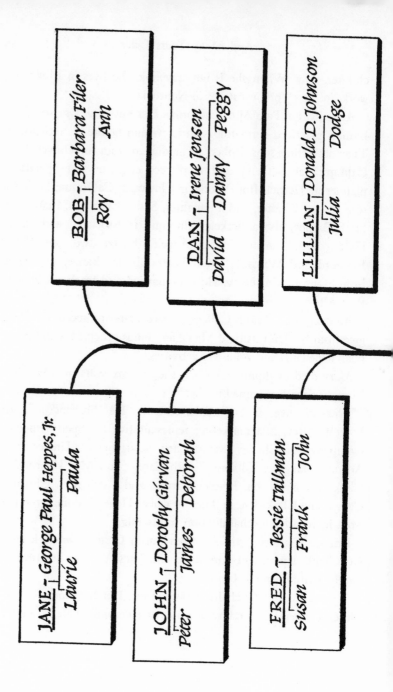

BOB - Barbara Filer
Roy   Ann

DAN - Irene Jensen
David   Danny   Peggy

LILLIAN - Donald D. Johnson
Julia   Dodge

JANE - George Paul Heppes, Jr.
Laurie   Paula

JOHN - Dorothy Girvan
Peter   James   Deborah

FRED - Jessie Tallman
Susan   Frank   John

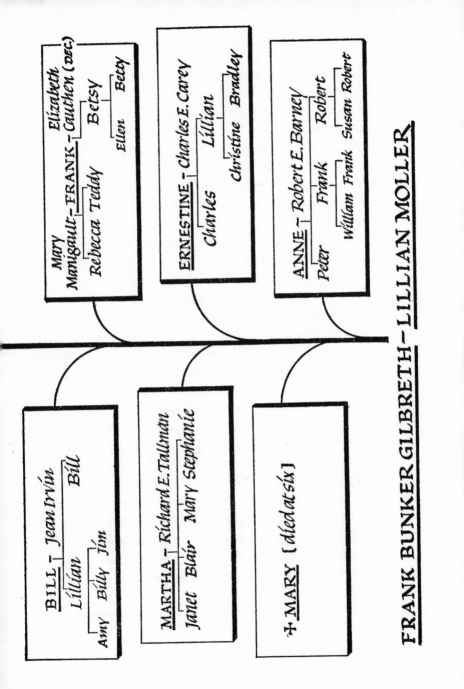

BILL ~ Jean Irvin
Lillian   Bill
Amy Billy Jim

MARTHA ~ Richard E. Tallman
Janet Blair Mary Stephanie

✝ MARY [died at six]

Mary
Manigault—FRANK—Gauthen (DEC)
Rebecca Teddy   Betsy
          Ellen   Betty

Elizabeth

ERNESTINE ~ Charles E. Carey
Charles   Lillian
     Christine Bradley

ANNE ~ Robert E. Barney
Peter   Frank   Robert
  William Frank Susan Robert

FRANK BUNKER GILBRETH—LILLIAN MOLLER

Company, Inc., wholesale lumber brokers and manufacturers. They have four daughters: Janet Wallace, who attends Whitman College in Walla Walla, Washington, and Martha Blair, Mary Elizabeth, and Stephanie Scott, who are in school in Chehalis.

Martha, after graduation from Douglass College in New Brunswick, New Jersey, worked for the American Telephone and Telegraph Company in New York, the Montclair public school system, and the Montclair Public Library. She now devotes herself to family and local activities.

Frank lives in Charleston, South Carolina, where he is assistant publisher of two daily newspapers. His older daughter, Betsy, has two daughters, Betty and Ellen. After his first wife died, he remarried and now has two young children, Teddy and Rebecca. He attended St. John's College in Annapolis for a year and was subsequently graduated from the University of Michigan. He first moved to Charleston in 1934, worked for the Associated Press in Raleigh, North Carolina, and New York City, and moved back to Charleston in 1947. During World War II he served in the Navy.

Bill lives in Villanova, a suburb of Philadelphia. He is vice-president and general manager of the Skelton Oil Company, a subsidiary of Gulf Oil Corporation. He is a mechanical engineer from Purdue and served in the Navy in World War II. His wife, Jean, was a Purdue girl and she now works for the Red Cross. Their son, Bill Jr., is a student at Haverford School in Haverford, Pennsylvania. Their daughter, Lillian, named for her grandmother, also attended Purdue. Lill is married to Jim Holmwood, an industrial engineer from Purdue, who is a sales engineer for Esso, making him a competitor as well as a son-in-law. Lill and Jim have three children: Jim IV, Billy, and Amy.

Lillian lives in Wilmington, Delaware. Her husband, Donald

Vasiliu

243

Dodge Johnson, is in the tariff division of E. I. du Pont de Nemours and Company. They have a son, Dodge Jr., and a daughter, Julia. Dodge, married to Martha Niepold, is a graduate of Princeton (his father's alma mater) and is now studying for his doctorate at the University of North Carolina at Chapel Hill. Julie graduated from Smith, as did her mother, and from the Katharine Gibbs School.

Lillian is most interested in antiques and volunteer work.

Fred lives in Larchmont, New York, and is an organization consultant with I.B.M. in New York City. In 1943 he married Jessie Blair Tallman, a graduate of Barnard College. She is the sister of Richard Tallman, Martha's husband. His daughter, Susan, attends Smith College and his boys, Frank II and John, are in the public schools. He graduated as a mechanical engineer from Brown University, served in the 8th Air Force in Europe, and worked for the management consulting firm of McKinsey and Company in New York for thirteen years before joining I.B.M. in 1958.

Dan lives in Montclair, New Jersey. A graduate of the University of Pennsylvania's Wharton School of Finance and Commerce, he is president of D. B. Gilbreth and Company, heavy machinery exporters, and of Intercontinental Maritime, Inc., exporters of yachting equipment. He was in the Navy in World War II. He is married to the former Irene Jensen. Daughter Peggy, '63 alumna of Northwestern University, is doing graduate work in psychology at Purdue. Sons Danny and David are students at Mt. Hebron School in Montclair.

John lives in Upper Montclair, New Jersey. Jack graduated from Princeton University, later served in the Navy in World War II, and has worked in various fields of industrial engineering. He is now coordinator of labor standards for Mobil International Oil Company in New York City. He and his wife, the former Dorothy Girvan, have three children: Peter, James, and Deborah.

Bob lives in Franklin, New Hampshire, where he is a teacher and principal of the local junior high school. He is married to the former Barbara Filer. They have two children: Ann and Roy. Barbara has worked as a bookkeeper, engineering aide, and schoolteacher.

Jane lives in Palo Alto, California. Her husband, George Paul Heppes Jr., is one of two owner-operators of a local restaurant called St. Michael's Alley. Paul is a graduate of Williams College. Daughters Laurie and Paula are students in the Palo Alto schools.

Jane has been active in the Junior League, Girl Scouts, and the Community Volunteer Office. Her interests are spectator sports, reading, and writing.